PHILADELPHIA REBEL

With Best wishes
Clara Jaeger

PHILADELPHIA REBEL

The Education of a Bourgeoise

CLARA JAEGER

GROSVENOR

RICHMOND VA LONDON
MELBOURNE OTTAWA WELLINGTON

First published 1988
GROSVENOR USA,
PO Box 8647
Richmond, Va 23226

GROSVENOR BOOKS
54 Lyford Road,
London, SW18 3JJ

21 Dorcas Street,
South Melbourne,
Victoria 3205, Australia

302–141 Somerset St. West
Ottawa, Ontario K2P 2HI
Canada

PO Box 1834, Wellington,
New Zealand

US Trade Distributor:
M & B Fulfillment Service Inc.,
540 Barnum Avenue,
Bridgeport, Conn. 06608

Designed by Blair Cummock
Cover design by Cameron Johnson

Library of Congress Catalog
Pre-assigned Card Number 87–082189

British Library Cataloguing in Publication Data
Jaeger, Clara
   Philadelphia Rebel: the education
   of a bourgeoise.
   1. Christian life
   I. Title
   248.4   BV4501.2

   ISBN 1–85239–502–8

Phototypeset in Sabon by Input Typesetting Ltd., London, S.W.19, England
Printed and bound by McNaughton & Gunn, Michigan, USA

Front cover: l to r Theodore Dreiser, Clara Jaeger, Frank Buchman.

TO BILL, FREDERIC AND JOAN

ACKNOWLEDGEMENTS

Special thanks to Mary Lean who took a long manuscript and with great skill and imagination honed it into shape. Equally I want to thank Hugh Nowell who supported me through the various versions the book passed through, as too Elizabeth Locke.

I want to give thanks as well to Terry and Demie Blair, Steve and Catherine Dickinson, Michael Henderson and Stuart Smith, all of whom gave invaluable suggestions.

Particular thanks go to Peter and Margaret Sisam for undertaking the design of the photographs and for their conception and arrangement of them.

Thanks too go to Barbara Guilbride, Pat Jones and Sue Bolton who did so much typing.

I want to thank Doë Howard and Angela Owbridge who were the first to urge me to launch out on such a personal story.

My two brothers, Warner and Arthur, are so much a part of this story and so dear to me, along with their wives, Dorothy and Mary, that I would like to thank them here for their love and trust throughout the writing.

FOREWORD

WHAT I HAVE WANTED to write: to try to describe only a little bit the journey of an ordinary human being through what we call life, to try to show how there is in most a hunger for meaning, to try to show how we are all pocked with blind places, keep falling on our faces, hurting and being hurt. Some of us have an underlying dread, even terror. Some can be, like the hare, on the run from the hounds of heaven and of hell, and in the end, from the facing up to death.

And in us often is a rebellion at this arrangement, and the sadness – because rebellion or no, we will have to submit.

So, could there be a meaning?

If there is a Prime Creator, then the whole scene is transformed in an instant. Sadness and pain and terror can become gifts, an education of the heart and soul.

I

'DID YOU COME for the publicity?'

I was sitting on the edge of the bed in a New York hotel room, my questioner opposite, occupying the one armchair.

'Of course not,' I exclaimed vehemently. The implication shocked me.

It was October 1931. My companion was Theodore Dreiser, then at the height of his fame as a novelist. He had just celebrated his sixtieth birthday, with wide coverage in the press. I was twenty-two, from a Philadelphia Quaker family.

Within twenty-four hours he had offered me a secretarial job, helping him with his next book.

So began my four-year association with the controversial writer. It seemed to offer me the chance to break free. Yet the search for freedom was to continue all my life.

The story opens in Germantown, Pennsylvania . . .

1909–14 – Germantown, Philadelphia, Pennsylvania

When thirteen families from Krefeld, Germany, arrived in the New World on October 6, 1683, they settled in a place where 'the water was pure and the air was clean.' Among them was one of my ancestors on my father's side, Jan Luken. Daniel Pastorious was another arrival at that time, and he it was who founded Germantown.

When I was born in 1909, Germantown, ten miles north from the center of Philadelphia, was a quiet suburb of comfortable gray fieldstone houses. A good deal of the architecture was 'colonial' – white painted porticos, fan lights, wooden shutters, and on some of the newer, grander houses, porte cochères.

In the eighteenth century, Germantown was a country retreat for Philadelphians suffering from the stifling summer heat and humidity of the city. George Washington and Benjamin Franklin set up summer residences there while the Constitution of the newly-born United States was being hammered out in the city. It was in Philadelphia, a decade earlier, that the Declaration of Independence was read on 4 July 1776. There too Betsy Ross ran up the first American flag with its stars and stripes; and there George Washington was elected first president of the new country.

Philadelphia was occupied by the British in the winter of 1777–8, while Washington's army lay at Valley Forge, twenty miles away. When Washington attempted to dislodge the British, he was stopped at Germantown and a fierce battle ensued. Two of Germantown's best-known houses, Wyck House and Clivedon, were battered by British canon-fire in the process. Then a thick fog came down and the Americans were forced to retreat in some confusion.

School House Lane, where I was born, was the front line of the British defense during this period. Its cross streets were all named after patriots of the American Revolution. First from our house was Morris Street, named for the man who more than any other financed the war against England; then Pulaski Street, named for a Polish general who joined Washington's army; then Wayne Avenue, after General 'Mad' Anthony Wayne, another of Washington's generals and our collateral ancestor; then Green Street, after another General. School House Lane itself stretched from German-town Avenue in the east – once, so they said, an Indian trail – to the Schuylkill River in the west.

My father loved American history. As I walked these streets during the first twenty years of my life, his enthusiasm rubbed off on me and nurtured a sense of patriotism in my heart.

I was born in a twin house with three storys, an attic and a front and back yard. A ten minute's walk from our house took us down into Fairmount Park, the 'largest landscaped city park in the world,' or so we were always told. Through it ran a beautiful creek, almost a small river, with an Indian name, the Wissahickon. Large sections of the park were like small forests.

In my early childhood, automobiles were still a rarity on the streets. Most Sunday afternoons, Mr. Frederick Strawbridge, a prominent Philadelphia merchant, would pass our house in his four-in-hand, bound for the Park and a drive along the Wissahickon.

My mother was a birthright Quaker, with ancestors going back to 1658 when, as we were told, William Warner, a captain in Cromwell's army, fled the threatening Restoration in England and settled in a 'dugout' on the west side of the Schuylkill River. He later built a beautiful house called Blockley in the rich farmland of Chester County.

My mother's four sisters, parents and many relatives were all Quakers. We all said 'thee' and 'thy' to each other, although my father was an Episcopalean. He was devoted to the Quakers, but found their form of worship – sitting in silence until 'the Spirit led someone to speak' – alarming. Early in their engagement, my mother took him to a Quaker meeting and, to his intense embarrassment, rose and spoke. After that my father persuaded her to join the Episcopal Church, where the Book of Common Prayer guaranteed a safe framework for all utterances.

Philadelphia was also a center for cricket. In the late nineteenth century, thousands would turn out to watch such matches as 'The Gentlemen of Philadelphia vs Mr Warner's English Team.' Two of my uncles played the game, and the city had four clubs.

* * * * *

From those first five years, what do I remember? Becoming very angry with my nurse when I was about three; stamping and throwing my hairbrush on the floor when she struggled to curl my long hair by brushing it round her finger . . . I remember being taken to visit Grandmother and Grandfather Clark in a place called Conshohocken, across the river from

Germantown. Big Bridget, my nurse, took me on the train. I wandered into the stable where the two carriages were kept. It had such an interesting smell and there were all kinds of harness hanging on the walls.

On my return, I found I had a baby brother, called Warner. Unlike me, he was a good baby and rarely cried. I was always getting into a tantrum and having to be spanked. Early on I began to boss Warner – I had so many ideas about games to play.

Then, in September 1914, I started kindergarten at Germantown Friends School, where my mother, aunts and grandmother had all studied. It was co-educational. For the next fourteen years I was to walk the two miles there and back every day, in all sorts of weather. In those early years I carried a wicker lunch basket with a sandwich in it.

June 1915 – Germantown

The first roses are just coming into bloom in our garden. I have a small private plan. My teacher is slim and blonde and blue-eyed and has quite won my heart. I pick three pink roses for her and carry them to school, placing them on her desk. My heart pounds in eager anticipation of the moment when she will discover that I have brought them to her.

Our little class gather around her. Almost fainting with excitement, I watch her pick up the roses. 'And who brought me these lovely roses?' she asks, gazing out over her little group. I am just about to speak, when another little girl jumps up, and calmly claims the glory. I am so astonished and shocked, that I simply close my mouth and sit down. I never tell anyone about it.

1916 – Germantown

Another baby brother, Arthur, has arrived, and I am now in first grade and learning to read.

Spring 1917 – Whitford

Great excitement. My parents take us into the country to look at a place we may rent for the summer, in a small rural community called Whitford in the Chester Valley.

One of our many uncles has a motor car and he drives us. We stop several times along the dusty road to pay toll. When we pass carriages, the horses jump and snort in terror.

We arrive at a yellow house with green shutters, sitting directly on the road. Near the front door there is a white stone mounting-block to help the ladies onto their horses, and a tall privet hedge hides the grounds from the road. The house dates from the early eighteenth century.

Inside we find beautiful, cool rooms, each with a large fireplace. The fireplace in the living-room makes us fairly gasp. It is tall enough for a man to stand up in, and about six feet in length. An iron door opens in the right-hand side of the chimney, leading into a vast oven. There are large wooden beams at intervals all along the ceiling.

But the greatest wonder is discovering that a real stream runs the length of the four-acre grounds – a beautiful, sparkling brook, about four feet wide. Long grasses and irises grow along the banks. We fly down to look at it.

July 1917 – Whitford

We have moved into our house in the country and the days just aren't long enough to experience all the delights that are ours. It is a lush, green, peaceful world. Warner and I spend hours squatting beside our own little brook, among the reeds, irises and tiger lilies. We have made a fleet of wooden boats, and sail them endlessly.

Across the three-barred wooden fence, which separates our lawns from the meadow, a large herd of Guernsey cows is grazing. Several of them come to look at us playing in our brook. We climb the fence and scratch their ears filled with fuzzy fur, trying to avoid their wet, rough tongues. We feed them branches from the willow trees that stand on either side of the brook.

The cows are very clean and smell slightly of mint. Among all the brown and white ones, there is one black and white – a Holstein. Her name is Mary-me-Ann, and we hear from the farmer that she gives fourteen quarts of milk a day.

*   *   *   *   *

Most of the conversation now seems to be about the war, and the Kaiser. There is a large vegetable garden at the back of our house beside the chicken run. There are no men available to take care of the garden because they have gone to the war, so one day two young women arrive, dressed in khaki plus-fours, and spend the day working in the garden. More young women suddenly appear on the dusty white road beyond our hedge. The road has developed ruts and holes and the women attack them with a steam-roller and picks and shovels.

Our mother drives four miles several times a week to roll bandages for the Red Cross. All the women are knitting for the soldiers.

In the evening we can hear people singing: *It's a long way to Tipperary* and *There's a long, long trail a-winding*. It sounds very sad.

October, 1917 – Germantown

I have started second grade. My report for the first month shows all As and Bs. I love to read and I manage arithmetic.

We have also started dancing classes. We do just as we are told by the teacher, while our mothers sit and watch. We like to slide on the polished floor. Most of us are eight years old. Whenever the teacher tells the boys to choose partners, they make a dash for the prettiest girls. I am not one of these, though I usually get a partner. This kind of thing begins to create in me a sense of self-doubt and unease.

March 1918 – Germantown

A very bad day. I begin to experience a taste of the harshness of reality and become aware of the loneliness and fear that lurk in shadowy corners. A small person is being launched into the great world – without being told very much about it.

For the last dance of the season we are asked to wear fancy dress. I am to be Betsy Ross, the clever seamstress who made the first American flag. Alas, I am in no way a natural beauty and my dear mother, it seems to me rather impatiently, pulls down onto my head what I sense immediately, with every fiber of my already feminine soul, to be a most unbecoming cap.

Mother must have labored hard and long at her sewing machine and my tears and rebellion must sorely try her patience, but I know all too well, as I gaze in the mirror, that I am doomed if I wear this cap. This time my mother's will prevails. She takes me firmly by the hand and carts me off to the dance, where I am left to make my way as best I can.

Comes the opening dance and the usual mad rush of little boys for partners. There are some lovely little girls in beautiful, gauzy costumes – fairies and little queens, what I would have liked to have been.

No small youth comes for me, and I sit swinging my legs, panic growing in my stomach. Two dances go by, and then a partner approaches me; but he is the class 'fool,' a poor, gangling, awkward child. Summoning up my courage, I rise and curtsy to his bow, and we are off.

Finally the afternoon comes to an end. I have spent most of it sitting in a corner. There were not enough boys to go around.

Mother takes me home, but neither of us say anything about the afternoon. I want to forget it. Is Mother unaware of my small ordeal or does she suffer quietly for me?

July 1918 – Whitford

Dad has been building us a boat in the back of the barn. She is a flat-bottomed boat, with a square bow and stern. Dad calls her a 'scow.' He asks us what color we would like her painted and we choose bright blue with a red trim. The oarlocks are fitted and we carry her in triumph down to the wide meadow stream for the launching.

Now we are busy all day with our boat. In some places the creek is quite deep, almost six feet directly in front of the dam. The only thing I don't like are the crayfish, which I have been told will bite your toes. I keep a wary eye out for them when I am wading in the deep weeds along the bank.

We are rarely out of our bathing suits and become very brown in the bright, hot sun. The cows come and look at us in our boat, standing beside the water chewing the cud.

*   *   *   *   *

There has been a fierce thunderstorm, followed by a day of torrential rain. The creek has risen almost a foot, spilt over into the meadow, and become a rushing river. One of the cows has lost a calf. She stands under a tree beside the creek and moos loudly all day and all night, until the farmer comes and leads her away.

And then the water goes down, leaving the long grass along the side of the creek flat and streaked with mud. The sun is out again, bright and hot, the air steamy. Circling around and around in the sky are huge black buzzards. They suddenly glide down and begin eating the carcass of the baby calf which was washed up on the bank when the water receded. We watch, horrified yet fascinated. The feasting goes on for almost a week. The place begins to smell and the farmer comes and takes away what is left of the carcass.

September 1918 – Germantown

Back to school again and now in third grade. The smell of the new lead pencils is now a familiar one, especially when they are put through the pencil sharpener.

Life turns out to be rather pleasant this year. I am used to the routine. I am beginning to take a bit of leadership. Already most of us are labeling our classmates and placing them on different rungs of the success ladder. There are two queens at the top: one a pretty redhead to whom the handsomest boys pay court; the other, Anna, a shrewd, wise, fun-loving girl, comes from one of the leading families of Philadelphia. I, and a good many others, set out to win her favor. I discover I can do it by thinking up ways to get a laugh to relieve the monotony of the classroom. I don't mind playing the fool and being sent out of the room by the teacher.

We are all bursting with health and energy, and we soon organize ourselves into a club. We meet every afternoon when school is finished and play violent games of Prisoner's Base and Old Witch, until I am ready to drop. We take turns in each other's houses, but by far the best place to meet is Anna's. Her large, brown-painted house, with its turrets, chimneys and porte cochère, sits in a rolling estate. There is a wood behind the lawns, a tennis ourt, stables and beautiful gardens. Here we can run until we are exhausted.

*   *   *   *   *

I take a short cut home from school, kicking my way through thick piles of brown, red and golden leaves. The leaves are falling everywhere, like silent rain, and covering the sidewalk. People are raking them up and burning them in great piles so that the air is pungent and sweet from the smell, but they still keep falling.

Suddenly a band of boys come shouting and yelling around the corner. Their rough manner alarms me. I skirt the pushing, shoving group, receiving some jeers and laughter as I timidly make my way along the edge of the pavement.

They don't molest me. I am disturbed, nevertheless, by more than my fear of the boys' roughness – I sense another world perched on the borders of my protected and privileged one.

November 1918 – Germantown

My mother has gone out of her mind. As we come down to breakfast, the air is shattered with a bedlam of noise. Factory whistles are blowing, bells are ringing, horns hooting, people shouting all up and down the street. Mother, a person of much dignity, is running around on the front lawn and shouting and crying like a young girl. She picks us up and swings us through the air. She kisses Dad right in front of everyone. We finally understand that an armistice has been declared and that the war with Germany is over.

* * * * *

The next day we hear that it was a false announcement, but finally, on November 11th, the armistice is signed. We hear also that one of Dad's cousins has been killed in France – at Belleau Wood.

We are taken into town to see the parade, setting out very early because of the crowds. We go to the tall building where Dad has his law office and sit in the window for ages, looking down on thousands of people jamming the street. Flags are everywhere. Then at last the bands heading the parade come into view and the noise is deafening. It is hard for us to understand why our parents are so stirred up.

Christmas Eve 1918 – Germantown and Conshohocken

We are packing the car to drive to Grandmother's for Christmas. It is just beginning to snow and promises to turn into a real storm. The air is bitterly cold and the sky lowering. We are very excited. Mother and Dad sit in front, we three in the back with a rug to keep us warm. Dad has put up the isinglass curtains to keep out some of the bitter wind.

We drive westward, just as the winter evening begins to close in. We go along an old turnpike which is full of history, Dad pointing out the familiar landmarks of the revolutionary war.

We turn off the pike in our small car and drive onto a narrow country road that plunges up and down the rolling hills. We pass through woods. Only the oak trees still hold their brittle, brown leaves, and the pines and hemlocks their green needles.

It is dark now and snowing quite hard. My father peers anxiously through the windshield. Then in another twenty minutes we are driving down the wide main street of Conshohocken, turning suddenly into a carriageway. The church bells are ringing. The town seems full of church bells.

We arrive at Grandmother's – a large clapboard house with a long porch. We rush to the front door, which is decorated with a magnificent wreath tied with wide red ribbons.

Everything this grandmother does is done with style. Even to our childish eyes, the high quality of the red satin speaks.

We impatiently push open the door and spring into the glorious warm hall, rushing out of the bitter cold. Grandmother, small and stout and solid, embraces us; so does a maiden aunt. Cousins and uncles and aunts appear from the doorways. There is a delicious smell from the wood fire burning in the library and from the balsam branches hanging everywhere.

I am taken up the long carpeted stair and shown my room. Although I have seen it before, its luxury quite bowls me over – the huge black walnut double bed, the dressing table with long mirror, the chaise longue, and the adjoining bath with the most wonderful smell of special soap. Grandmother's maid helps me take off my things. She is glad to have children in the house.

I stop and stare a moment at the brass plate fastened to the wall with a row of buttons that switch the electric lights on and off. We do not have electricity at home, only gas. I summon up my courage and push one of them. A bright light flashes on behind a frosted glass globe. It seems a wonder to be able to live with such a thing.

But there is one ordeal connected with a visit to Grand-mother's. To get downstairs, I must pass through a sitting-room adjoining my bedroom. Hanging on the wall is a large engraving in an oak frame. I draw near and stare and stare, in spite of my dread.

The picture shows a thick forest. In the foreground, hiding behind a tall tree, is a couple, presumably man and wife: the man in coonskin cap, fringed jacket and trousers, carrying a long rifle; the woman bare-headed, with a shawl pulled around her shoulders and a look of terror on her face. She seems to be pressing against the tree trunk for safety and shelter; and no wonder, because in the distance, and closing in, I can see Indians, also carrying rifles with fearful toma-hawks in their hands as well. They appear to be running.

What will be the fate of this pioneer couple, alone in the vast forest, with so many advancing upon them? Nothing can prevent detection, I am sure. My lip trembles. I can feel myself being chased, something closing in on me behind my shoulder even as I stand before the picture. I turn and hurry away downstairs to the warmth and love of the family gathered there.

Christmas Day 1918 – Conshohocken

I lie in my huge bed under the warm quilt listening to the church bells. They are ringing out Christmas carols. It is incredibly beautiful. I feel like crying, yet I am wildly happy.

At six o'clock there are stockings to open; at eight o'clock there is breakfast; at ten o'clock there is church; at one o'clock there is a huge dinner. Grandmother leads the procession into the dining-room. She sits at one end of the table and we fill in all down the long length. There are sixteen of us. Grandmother is a true gourmet and serves lavish menus. The turkey is so large that the maids can scarcely carry it. Dessert is a mountain-mold of meringue with ice cream in layers. When it finally comes, we can hardly see Grandmother as she serves, hidden from view behind this Everest of a sweet.

We finally stagger back into the library and sit around the fire. The men light up their cigars. Two of the cousins have just returned from the war in France. They are the center of attention. I am very much in awe of them when I hear where they have been, and sit quietly listening.

February 1919 – Germantown

I have made great friends with my other grandmother, Mother's mother. She has invited me to come and visit her as often as I like. My two grandmothers are very different from each other – and so are their houses.

Nana, as her thirteen grandchildren call her, is not worldly. Her husband, now dead for ten years, was a manufacturer. They were leaders in the Germantown Quaker Meeting. I have heard many stories about them and their five girls: the independent way they lived, with little money, yet enjoying life immensely – and with many beaus calling at the house!

The most important thing about Nana is her strong faith in God. She has thirteen Bibles in her house.

I walk up the flagstone path, up the porch steps and open the heavy oak front door. It is never locked. Not even at night. Nana says they have nothing any burglar would want, which isn't quite true, because there is a good deal of silver on the sideboard for one thing and lots of blue and white Canton china all over the dining-room. But there isn't any money around and there are no jewels, since the Quakers feel jewelry is worldly and leads to vanity.

I run up the broad oak staircase, and there at the head of the stairs is Nana's sitting-room. It is plainly furnished, but the walls are covered with dozens of photographs of every member of her large family.

She is very handsome: tall and stately. Although she is

in her sixties, there is no gray in her hair, which she wears plaited and wound into a crown on the top of her head.

When Nana was at our school, two generations back, the artist Joseph Pennell was one of her classmates. Family gossip has it that Pennell called Nana the most beautiful woman he had ever seen! Quakers were supposed to be free from vanity, but I remember many a talk among my relatives on the subject of physical beauty, or the lack of it.

We often read the Bible together when I visit Nana – the stories of Ruth, Samuel, Elijah – and this afternoon is no exception. When I get home I decide to read the Bible straight through. I start out eagerly enough but finally peter out at Second Kings. Then Nana gives me *The Story of the Bible*. This does the trick and I go right through from beginning to end – four times. God becomes very real to me. The story of the Crucifixion I find shattering.

June 1919 – Germantown

It is the last day of school for this year and I almost explode for joy. It is one of those marvelous June days.

Walking to school I skip along – past gardens ablaze with roses, past black iron fences draped in rambling rose vines and honeysuckle, underneath an archway of soft new green made by the tall trees.

Tomorrow we are to go for a visit to our family hotel, 160 miles north.

In 1899, Nana's husband, William Warner, took his wife and his five little girls to a place called Eagles Mere in the mountains of Pennsylvania. In those days it was a true wilderness with miles of forests stretching out on every hand with a little jewel of a lake nestled among the trees. Across the lake from the hotel where they were staying, William Warner noticed a commanding eminence known as Cyclone Hill, which had been stripped of its virgin timber by a hurricane in the year 1892. He had the inspiration that he should purchase the hill and build a modern and comfortable summer hotel where whole families could come and enjoy a happy, healthy holiday. There would be a stable full of beautiful horses, and family prayers for all who chose to attend.

He raised the money without difficulty, and in eight short months that dream came true. In June 1900, the Crestmont Inn opened its doors. And there *was* a stable full of beautiful horses, as well as an excellent chef.

The Inn's peak season is July and August, so the family goes there in June and September. There are so many Warner relations who want to go to Eagles Mere tomorrow that Nana is hiring a private Pullman car. It will be attached to the regular train leaving the Reading Terminal at eight a.m.

June 1919 – Eagles Mere

At three o'clock, we arrive at the little town of Muncy. We all scramble out of the big train and climb on to a funny little narrow gauge train that is waiting there for us, puffing and steaming, with smoke pouring out of its tall wide-topped chimney. Inside, it has red velour seats and stained glass windows in blue, gold, green and red. The train takes us up Eagles Mere Mountain, 2,200 feet above sea level. The track runs through heavy woods; the branches of the trees brush against our windows. The speed is six miles an hour; our uncles keep jumping off the train, running alongside and jumping back again onto the wooden platform outside the car.

Suddenly we have arrived. There is the lake, bright blue and sparkling. We pull into a small station. Lined up beside the track are rows of long carriages, each with a team of horses, drivers and footmen who shout out the name of the hotel their carriage serves. There are six different hotels – only ours is high above the lake, with its own mountain-top view, it is said, of twenty-two counties.

We enter the carriage by steps at the back and take our places on the long seats which run lengthwise along both sides.

✳ ✳ ✳ ✳ ✳

The Eagles Mere lake must be one of the most beautiful anywhere. It is said to be a glacier lake, fed by springs eighty feet down. Here it sits: a mile long, a quarter of a mile across and three miles of shoreline. Hemlock trees, pine, giant rhododendrons and mountain laurel frame its shores. In many places, the laurel and hemlock grow right down to the water. At the far end there is a white sandy beach. There are boat houses, a dock and a float with diving boards.

The mountain laurel is in bloom. It leans in masses of delicate shell pink blooms over the green-blue water.

*   *   *   *   *

Nana asks me if I will row her to the bathing beach, and I accept joyfully. Nana takes her parasol, knitting bag and several books, and we start off down the steep path from the hotel. The path is reddish brown earth, and weaves its way through long, fragrant grasses. Growing among the grasses are daisies and buttercups and what we call Devil's paint-brush – a small, furry, bright orange-reddish flower which lights up the grass like bits of fire.

When the boatman sees Nana approaching, he gets out her boat and slides it into the water. Nana's boat is quite grand – steady and wide with comfortable wicker backrests. She has plenty of cushions as well, and when the boat is in the water, she takes her place among the cushions, putting up her parasol. I take my place at the oars, facing her; the boatman gives us a shove and we head for the beach, a mile away.

I am wiry and strong and used both to rowing and paddling a canoe. I love being in the water and enjoy upsetting a canoe and climbing back in again.

I get a rhythm and row the large boat, blissfully happy. It is early in the season, and the boat smells strongly of its new coat of varnish.

September 1919 – Eagles Mere

Back again; today we went on an all-day hike through the woods. There are trails marked out by colored arrows on stones and tree-trunks along the way. We have been sternly warned never to go off the paths into the thick unmarked forest. Some of the giant hemlocks in one part are primeval.

About forty of us start off, mostly grown-ups, but a small band of us cousins as well. These hikes are very popular. The guests sign up for them; lunches are provided by the hotel.

We walk in single file, singing. One of the hikers is a young man with a clear ringing tenor voice. He has come to work in the hotel office for the summer. I run and skip along, listening to him singing, and something slightly disturbing begins to creep into my consciousness. The young clerk's name is Stephen. He is tall, with dark, curly hair and bright blue eyes. Something in the warmth of his voice stirs me. We sing the war songs, all the familiar ones I used to hear when I was small, especially *There's a long, long trail awinding.*

We have been hiking for several hours, have had our box lunch, and it is now late afternoon. We have left the woods and have come out into a field filled with golden-rod and purple asters. We walk along a stream, sometimes directly in it, with our shoes and socks on. The sun is getting low in the west. My legs are beginning to feel very tired . . . Suddenly, Stephen picks me up in his arms and swings me onto his shoulder. I ride the rest of the way home, quite overcome.

*   *   *   *   *

I have just had a large breakfast of oatmeal and hot cakes with maple syrup. It is quite cool today, one of those snappy September mornings when the air is full of tang and something electric. The steam heat is turned on in the hotel and makes banging noises in the pipes and radiators. A large log fire crackles and roars in the lobby. The place smells wonderfully fragrant from the smoke and from the men's cigars and pipes.

I feel lazy for a change and decide to curl up by the fire and read. I want to enjoy this fragrant warmth. Different members of the family are around, talking to the guests and among themselves.

But there is this other thing creeping into my protected world. I can hear Stephen's voice as he speaks to the guests from the front desk. I feel terribly shy, and afraid to look at him.

Last night, after the long hike, he went into the music room and played the piano and sang. He played ragtime; he knows so many songs. He laughed and smiled and looked at people as he played. He seemed to do it all so easily, and with such grace. I sat in a corner and stared and wondered, joining in with the songs. A crowd gathered around the piano, singing – we often do this in the evenings. Most of the men were wearing white flannels and white buckskin shoes. The women's dresses were filmy.

I felt like crying, I was so restless and stirred up. I am madly in love with Stephen.

October 1919 – Germantown

We are back at school and are taking two new difficult subjects: Latin and French. I am bored by both of them, and to pass the time I often show off to my friends and get them laughing. This means I am regularly sent to the cloakroom for misbehaving. I don't mind, except that it is even more boring having nothing to do but look at the rows of coats and hats.

November 1919 – Germantown

One of my friends has invited me to hear Paderewski. He is giving a concert at the Academy of Music. We have a box, just overlooking the stage. He comes on, a small old man with a halo of white hair. He sits at the piano and a great hush comes over the hall. He plays. I am only beginning to be awakened by music, but I am moved by the sight of this old man, by his aura of greatness, and I can feel the electricity in the air as three thousand people sit listening, spellbound. For one of his encores he plays the Minuet in G, a melody I myself have mastered!

February 1920 – Germantown

My monthly report card for the first time shows a C and a D. These are for French and Latin. My high record is slipping. I find it harder to study these days. There are so many things to think about and wonder about and dream about.

One afternoon we go on a bobsled ride. We meet at the stable at the edge of Fairmount Park. The snow on the street is at least twelve inches deep and it is still snowing. We all pile on board the long sled, about twenty-five of us. The horses wear bells on their harness. The driver sets off into the park and we head up the Wissahickon Drive, singing and shouting and sometimes pushing each other off into the snow.

As we glide along in the stinging, snowfilled, winter afternoon, the air is filled with the sound of sleighbells, of the horses' hooves, of the swish of the sled's runners, and of our shouts and laughter. Apart from these intrusions, the world is wonderfully hushed and muffled by the deep snow. The road winds through deep rock gorges, overhung with dark hemlock whose branches now bend and yield to their burden of snow. It is a wonderful green and white and gray world.

Soon we see the lights of Valley Green, an old inn standing beside the stream, dating from pre-revolutionary times, still waiting to welcome the traveller out of the cold as it must have done over 200 years ago. It is a low-eaved, white-painted building, with green wooden shutters, and smoke pouring from its chimney.

We waste no time in jumping from the sled and rushing

up the steps into the lamp-lighted interior. The doors are white, with heavy iron latches and hinges, the floorboards more than a foot wide. There is an open fire at one end of the room, and we are soon clustering around it with mugs of hot cocoa topped with marshmallows.

February 14th, 1920 – Germantown

I receive lots of valentines, beautiful ones. They are marvelous creations. How I do love beautiful things! I am unable to guess any of the senders. Every envelope is printed.

When we take in the milk bottles this morning, they are frozen stiff for at least three inches on the top. We put the frozen cream on our cereal and sprinkle it heavily with brown sugar. A wonderful taste.

June 1920 – Germantown

School is almost finished again. This year I have invitations to three houseparties; I am giving one myself at Eagles Mere, for six of my best friends. At each party, we are the same crowd of girls.

I have a new coat, a brown and white tweed, and a straw hat trimmed with red cherries.

June 1920 – Eagles Mere

My houseparty is a great success. My friends and I go wild with excitement, trying to do everything at once. Our high spirits earn us some rebuffs from my uncle, who is now in charge of the hotel.

Stephen is behind the desk again, I quickly discover, but I am too involved with my friends to do more than glance at him from time to time. I know he is not for me. My role is to adore from a distance. He still plays the piano and sings after dinner in the evenings. He also plays a lot of tennis and has a smashing serve. My friends and I also play in the mornings before taking the canoes to the beach.

June 1920 – Whitford

It is a baking hot day, so I am sitting in the parlour of our house. The dark green venetian blinds are let down over the windows to shut out the glare, but nothing can muffle the noise of the locusts singing away in the trees.

After our trip to Eagles Mere, my friends and I have started writing round-robin letters to each other. We have discovered a book about the American Revolution and are all reading it in our respective holiday places. It is highly romantic and makes the British out as very wicked. I have become an ardent rebel and would love to have been a spy for General Washington. I begin to feel proud of being an American.

July 4th, 1920 – Whitford

We have hung out the flag in front of our house. Dad has made a huge bowl of lemonade, large enough to last all day. It sits on a table on the veranda. There is a large block of ice floating in it. We are told we can drink as much as we want to.

We are also taking turns making peach ice cream on the kitchen porch: real peaches, real cream, made by churning around and around in a wooden container filled with salted ice crystals.

Dad has laid out a tennis court on the lawn on the other side of our brook, and I am becoming quite good at the game.

March 1921 – Germantown

Another new experience today. I have been introduced to the corner drug store and to chocolate marshmallow sundaes! What a discovery. I am going to buy one as often as I can. They cost fifteen cents – and my allowance is only twenty-five cents a week.

We are all passionately in love with Douglas Fairbanks. We go to see him in *Robin Hood* over and over again. I think I will faint away in ecstasy when I watch him courting Maid Marion. Now I am reading all the novels of Sir Walter Scott.

November 1921 – Germantown

I am twelve years old now. I have my long brown hair bobbed by the barber, Mr. Robinson, who comes to the house to cut my brothers' hair. The sound of his scissors squishing through my slippery, thick locks makes me shudder. I can almost feel it. The hair falls in long, fur-like lengths on the white sheet covering the carpet. When he has finished, I go down on my knees and pick up the pieces of hair. They seem to be almost alive. I find a shoe box in the cupboard to keep them in.

I am too busy enjoying life to worry about my looks. I have come to terms with the fact that I am not one of the very pretty girls, and if tempted to worry about it, I quickly turn my thoughts away. But I love pretty clothes.

This year we are to start in Miss Lockwood's famous dancing class, held on Friday evenings at the Philadelphia Cricket Club.

I dress rather nervously for the first evening. Dad drives me the five miles to the club and deposits me. The club house is jammed with boys and girls, most of whom I know. We line up and walk in, girls first, to be received by Miss Lockwood. A majestic-bosomed lady, shimmering in black jet and tulle, she is standing on an oriental rug placed to one side of the dance floor. Her hair is pale gold, and piled high on her head. She is wearing long white gloves.

As we each arrive before her, she holds out the fingers of her hand. We grasp them, bob a curtsy, then hurry away to the rows of chairs lined up around the wall, there to wait the favor of the boys who will choose us for partners. I am quite used to this routine by now; we are all quite philosophical about it. We know who is popular, who is second-best and who is hopelessly unattractive and ill-equipped. It's clear that you have to have something special if you want to keep from sinking to the bottom of the heap.

When the boys come to choose us they are wearing white gloves. This amuses us. We are still living in a world of games and mischief, and I for one don't take this particular dancing class too seriously.

February 1922 – Germantown

As soon as February comes around, we all begin noticing the arrival of the birds, keeping a list. My favorite is the brown thrasher. Next is the wood robin, whose heart-breakingly beautiful song floods over the lawn as the sun begins to go down. I especially love birds with sleek brown backs and spotted breasts.

On Sunday afternoons in the spring, Dad suggests bird walks. We go tramping down the street a couple of blocks and in about five minutes are in the park and making our way to some open fields, in search of the shy bluebird with his red breast. Dad says we have to keep very quiet and just lie in the grass until he appears.

Sometimes this bores me, and I get quite impatient, wishing I were back home reading a book by the fire. Warner, however, is just as keen as Dad, and suddenly the bluebird arrives. He alights on the wooden fence; for a moment we thrill to his beauty.

February 1922 – Germantown

Such a wonderful experience today. I go to the Walnut Street Theatre in town to see Walter Hampden in Cyrano de Bergerac. I am completely transported by the play. I weep for Cyrano. The scene where he sits as an old man in the garden of the monastery, while the leaves fall slowly down from the autumn trees, is almost more than I can bear. It is so sad, and so beautiful. It opens up a vista for my hungry heart – a vista of sacrifice and love and tenderness. I long to be able to comfort a man like Cyrano. For someone to deny himself for love of someone less worthy than himself . . . well, that is romance!

March 1922 – Germantown

We have a surprise in school today. Our English class is taken by a real Englishman. Our own teacher is round and balding, with gold-rimmed spectacles. So we are very interested to see him talking to a good-looking young man, fair-haired, with a rosy complexion. He is introduced to us as a visitor from England. As he comes forward and stands in front of the class, I think he looks much too young and shy to be a teacher. He says he will read selections from Keats and Wordsworth and begins with *Ode to a Nightingale*.

As soon as we hear his voice speaking those enchanted words, we become absolutely still. His cultured tones and carefully enunciated consonants transport us into a far-off world – an older world of style and awareness. We are charmed and transfixed. It is sheer music, music to the ear and to the soul. For thirty minutes, twenty-five rather grubby, restless young Americans sit quietly under his spell. When he finishes we want to rush forward and speak to him, but we sit humbly in our seats, too much in awe to say anything.

The stranger gives us a smile, a wave, then is gone.

July 1922 – Whitford

We have had our usual round of houseparties at the end of the school season, and I am glad to be back here at the Meadow House. This summer we have taken to sleeping out in a tent, which Dad has put up beside the stream. I settle

A collateral ancestor, General Anthony Wayne, served under George Washington in the War of Independence. He fought the British at Brandywine and Germantown. His daring capture of Stony Point in 1779 made him a national hero.

Grandfather Charles Heber Clark, age 19, in the Army of the Potomac. He later took part in the Battle of Gettysburg, 1863.

My parents, Frederic Clark and Elizabeth
Warner, on their engagement

Beloved grandmother, Nana, 'very
handsome, tall and stately'

With my baby brother, Warner

On the bridge over the brook at Whitford – Warner and Arthur with our dog, and cousins

'Dad shooting the rapids on the Susquehanna River near Harrisburg'

'The summer has almost gone – so quickly. It has been hot, and I have lived in my bathing suit.'

down inside the tent with its canvas smell, but soon I take my blanket outside and fall asleep looking up at the stars.

*　　*　　*　　*　　*

Four of my friends come for a weekend. We spend practically the whole time swimming in the pool in the creek. I have been diving off the raft and walking along with my hands on the bottom of the pool and my legs showing out of the water. We are five girls, and I have the bright idea of taking off my bathing suit while I do this trick. This causes a good deal of merriment, but unfortunately when five o'clock comes and it is time to return to the house, I can't find my suit anywhere. I dive and dive, and crawl along on the bottom of the creek, but no suit! What to do? The walk back to the house is at least a quarter of a mile through an open meadow in view of the road. Not one of us has brought any kind of wrap. We decide that one of my friends must go up to the house, tell my mother what has happened and return with some form of covering.

She goes and I wait anxiously in the water, which is beginning to feel cold.

It seems a long time before we see our emissary running down the meadow. She looks so small. Finally she arrives, holding out another bathing suit.

'What did she say?' we ask.

'She was very cross.'

I climb out onto the bank, shivering, and pull on the covering garment. Quite subdued, we walk slowly up to the house. My mother is waiting for me. She looks more than she says. We are sent off to dress for dinner.

I am used to my mother's disapproval. I know I am a trial to her. I also know how much my parents love me. I feel able to be headstrong and defiant with them while I am shy and overawed by the rest of the world.

September 1922 – Eagles Mere

Back here again. Last night some of us took canoes out after supper. There had been a glorious sunset. In the dusk we paddled slowly and silently, while the shadows deepened and the streaked and burning sky gradually turned to inky black. The wind died down, and the lake became as smooth as glass. An orange moon began to climb the heavens. We dipped our paddles gently into the quiet water and glided slowly along, sometimes stopping to drift. Then from across the lake came the sound of a banjo and people singing. The sound of the banjo and the moon and the sweet night made my throat tighten. I felt a fierce and violent longing for something – but I don't know what it is.

*   *   *   *   *

I am thinking of Stephen. I feel frightened and shy. I know he will marry some beautiful girl of his own age. I am just a child, and quite insignificant. He is always very kind to me. Adoring him from afar tinges my days with a hint of sadness. A breath of cold air seems to creep over my shoulder. I have a glimpse of a grown-up world, so different from mine which is mostly walled in against pain.

October 1922 – Germantown

I am so proud of my father. He is able to do so many things. He is a large man, six feet two inches, with broad shoulders. He and his two brothers grew up leading active, outdoor lives – hunting, fishing, sailing, camping, canoeing. We have a framed photograph of Dad shooting the rapids in his canoe on the Susquehanna River near Harrisburg.

The brothers also learned how to handle guns, and Dad has passed on this knowledge to my brothers, though so far they only have a beebee gun. Dad himself keeps a revolver in one of the drawers of his dresser. I see it every week when I help Mother put away the laundry.

26

When we are at Eagles Mere, Dad often takes us camping in a rather wild place called Hunter's Lake. We have to drive down a corduroy road to get there, then row across the lake to a clearing in the forest where we can pitch our tent. The first thing Dad does on camping trips is to get a fire going.

Hunter's Lake is rather eerie – especially after dark when the loon suddenly lets out his piercing, mournful cry, stabbing the silence like a warning, or a call for help. It makes me shiver and move closer to the fire.

And Dad is the one who takes charge of the dinner-table conversation. Warner and Arthur are usually bored by Dad's stories, but I am not. His father was Charles Heber Clark, who, at the end of the last century, was well-known in both England and America under his pen name of Max Adler. He was the author of several humorous books, and, according to Dad, one of them sold a million copies. Grandfather was also on the editorial staff of *The Philadelphia Evening Bulletin* for fifteen years.

Grandfather fought in the Civil War as a nineteen year-old in the Pennsylvania Militia. He was at the Battle of Gettysburg. His was not a warrior's nature, and, though he did what he felt he had to do, he found his time in the army an ordeal. We have a photograph of him, a tall, thin young man in the uniform of the Army of the Potomac, wearing a peaked cap and leaning on his long rifle, the bayonet protruding above his head.

So my father has a strong link through his own father with the Civil War. He can still feel critical of the Confederacy and of England. He says the British sided with the southern states not just because they wanted cotton for their mills in Lancashire, but also because they felt that the southern planters were the real aristocrats, more civilized and cultivated than the hard-driving, money-making Yankees. This irks my father.

And in the early nineteenth century, the British shamelessly stopped our ships and shanghaied the crews. This was because 42,000 British seamen deserted the navy during the war with France, many to sign on with American ships where life was not so rigorous.

All these opinions rub off on me and color my feelings about England.

Mother, on the other hand, is the quiet supporter, keeping everything running smoothly and keeping track of the pennies.

She often speaks of her childhood and of her love of dogs and horses. She teaches us how to house-train the series of dogs who become part of our family. Mother is a very practical person. She made her first dress when she was nine years old.

November 1922 – Germantown

I have been invited to join one of the social clubs in the city. I am only vaguely aware of 'Society'. Several of my friends have sisters who are debs, but I am not interested. My inclinations are rebellious and non-conformist.

Most of my friends give a dance during the winter season. Some hold them in country clubs, others in their own homes, if they are large enough. I go to all these dances – we all do.

I went to one last night. It was quite far out in the country. No one danced with me the first dance; the next two were all right but then I sat out three dances. Panic began to sweep over me. I went into the dressing room. I knew from experience that there would always be one or two wallflowers in there passing the time away as painlessly as possible. I exchanged wan smiles with the girl I found there.

I began to rage inside. My stomach felt tied in knots. I took my coat and slipped outside into the cold night. It was only ten o'clock. I had an hour to wait. Dad would come at eleven.

I walked in the grounds, my teeth chattering. There was a swimming pool, boarded over for the winter. I walked around and around it. I could hear the dance music pouring

28

out from the building. I loved hearing the tunes. Everyone I knew took this sort of thing for granted – and so did I. You were thrown into the water and expected to swim – or dance.

After a while, I heard the orchestra playing *Goodnight ladies*, then everyone clapping.

I walked back across the lawn and stood waiting near the entrance to the driveway to catch Dad as he turned in.

Sure enough, there was our small car, and Dad hunched over the steering wheel. Dear Dad – I could hardly wait to reach him. I ran towards the car shouting, 'Dad, Dad' . . . He shoved on the brakes, surprised to see me outside.

I climbed in beside him and he turned the car around.

He asked me if it had been a good dance.

'Fine,' I said, shivering in the dark and fighting back my tears.

Why couldn't I tell Dad how lost I felt and how unable to make my way?

*   *   *   *   *

I never tell Mother, either. They give me everything anyone could want, but they don't know how to discern what I am really feeling. Perhaps I am too clever at hiding it. I turn off the painful fears, like throwing a switch; pushing away the self-doubts and keeping as active as possible with the things I do know how to do.

February 1923 – Germantown

It is Sunday evening. We are all sitting around reading, except Dad. He is in the music room playing hymns on the piano. He sings as he plays.

I love these hymns. I have heard them as long as I can remember, but they always take me close to tears. I wonder *why* I am so easily stirred – anything beautiful seems to choke me up. I wish I wasn't that way. Other people seem to sail through things. I long to be the kind of person who appears to be in control and adequate.

I hear Dad singing: 'The King of Love my Shepherd is, whose goodness faileth never . . . I nothing lack if I am His, and He is mine forever . . .' and then at the end . . . 'And on His shoulder gently laid, and home rejoicing brought me.'

This is Jesus, the Son of God. Jesus is the Good Shepherd. He will look after us all, especially people who feel lost and afraid. I don't know how He will do this, but I know He will.

When I read about the crucifixion, I imagine the nails going into my own flesh. I feel I must open my heart to Christ's anguish, which He endured for me.

About this time I set up a small altar on my bedside table with two candles, a picture of Christ, a cross and a prayer book. Every night for about six months, I light the candles and kneel before the table to say my prayers.

*   *   *   *   *

I wonder about the profound inequalities I see in my own small world. We grow more and more conscious of the social ladder. On our ladder there are two or three beauties at the top, then the majority like myself, wandering up and down the middle, and then, at the bottom, those whom everyone ignores or is bored by, the ones who are snubbed every day.

October 1923 – Germantown

Mother has finally arranged for me to join the social club she was talking about last year; before I know what is happening, she tells me that I am to be initiated. She is to take me in to town and leave me at the Eagle in Wanamaker's store – a famous meeting place.

I don't know even what the word 'initiation' means.

We go to Wanamaker's and to the Eagle which stands in the center of the ground floor, under a great dome which reaches up to the roof. Two smartly dressed girls step forward and introduce themselves. There is a third girl with them, also about to be initiated. The first two explain that we are to act as if we did not know them; we are to do exactly as they say, but to walk a few yards behind them.

Mother has left meanwhile, and our first destination is the toy department of Wanamaker's. Here our two supervisors buy us each a tin horn, and in sharp tones command us to start blowing and not to stop until told to do so. Many a head turns to stare as we walk to the elevator, blowing our horns all the way. If ever we let up, a ferocious look from our guides is enough to start us off again. Out of the elevator, through the crowded store, and out onto Broad Street, packed now with lunchtime throngs, on we go, still blowing.

I am in the most intense distress, but fear of the overseers is stronger even than that of looking a fool. And so for the next thirty minutes, we make our noisy way through the city streets.

After what seems an age of mortification, our cheeks red with embarrassment, we arrive at a doorway and are led inside. I have long since lost any sense of location. We are directed up some narrow stairs, and I am put into a small room by myself and told to remove all my clothes with the exception of my under-drawers. I am then told I will be blindfolded and brought into a room containing both men and women!

My guides close the door and leave me alone. What to do? Once again, fear of these young women overcomes everything else. I have never openly resisted authority before, so I remove my clothes and sit down on a wooden chair, shivering and clasping my arms across my front.

The door opens again, a large handkerchief is tied over my eyes and I am led up some more stairs and told that I am in a room full of people. I can hear clapping and laughter; then someone puts a garment of some kind around my shoulders, the bandage is pulled from my eyes, and I am surrounded by any number of smiling, friendly young women, all wanting to shake my hand and congratulate me.

There are no men. It has all been a hoax. I am now 'in'!

But once I can get away from all this friendliness, I have

only one wish – to forget the whole idea of joining the club. I never want to see any of them again.

*   *   *   *   *

Mother and Dad have been talking a lot lately about buying a larger house. Finally, they find one that seems ideal. It is quite large, and sits on the corner of three streets, on a raised piece of ground about twenty feet above street level. The location means we have privacy and unblocked views. A steep driveway leads up to the front door made of heavy oak with a black iron grille. There is a nice lawn surrounding the house, and quite a few large trees.

When we go to see it, we are very excited. The house is full of fireplaces. Even the big, square front hall, with its oak panelling, has its own fireplace, as well as the dining-room, living-room and small sitting-room. Upstairs, the bedroom I am to have has four windows with window seats. I am enchanted and start day-dreaming immediately, curled up on one of the seats.

February 1924 – Germantown

Grandmother has invited me to join her in her weekly visit to the Friday afternoon concerts of the Philadelphia Orchestra in the Academy of Music. These concerts, given three times a week, have become a great event, largely because of the conductor, Leopold Stokowski, or 'Stokie' as we call him. This golden-haired, foreign-accented maestro has Philadelphia society eating out of his hand. He has tamed society ladies who, before his advent, were a law unto themselves, arriving late for concerts if it suited them, even talking!

But no longer. The doors are firmly shut the moment the lights go down; no late-comers are allowed, though I have seen, once or twice, people caught on their way to their seats just as Stokie is about to lift his hands for the overture! He turns and stares, waiting, while three thousand pairs of eyes watch for them to find their seats in the darkened auditorium. Nor does anyone dare cough. The slightest sound, and the conductor turns around on the podium and stares fixedly until there is absolute silence.

But it is worth it. I am transported by the great symphony orchestra. The air in the famous old academy is warm and perfumed, and the hall, with its tier upon tier of boxes, its gold and scarlet and cream interior, its cherubs, its crystal chandelier, its marvelous acoustics, is a temple of joy.

Then I suddenly discover Wagner. As the first bars of *The Valkyrie* blaze out I am shocked by the impact of the rich, sensuous, voluptuous sound – what a world it opens up. I am carried away on golden rivers, rosy clouds, tossed and transported. Can living really be like this – somewhere? At some time? Then I find *Siegfried's Journey to the Rhine*, and *Lohengrin* and finally excerpts from *Tristan*. The music speaks of an experience to be dreamed about and waited for. But the shimmering, golden, sometimes fierce sound can be experience enough; a warm and golden bath. I rest in dreams.

July 1924 – Whitford

Today Dad arrives back from town with a most wonderful surprise – a victrola! He unpacks it on the floor of the parlor. We three children squat beside it. Dad has bought four records to begin with: *Yes, we have no Bananas*; *Mr. Gallagher and Mr. Sheehan*; John McCormack singing *There's a Long, Long Trail Awinding*; and Alma Gluck and Louise Homer singing *Home Sweet Home*.

Oh, how happy we are. For days we want to do nothing but play these records over and over again. I think I will never tire of them. I do so love music. It excites and moves me and hints of wonderful worlds to be discovered.

Then Dad brings home *The Floridora Sextet* and some songs by Caruso.

Another school year is under way. It is all comfortably familiar. I have now been going to the same school for eleven years, with the same set of friends. Every year a few new students join our class. We assess them carefully and shrewdly, coming as they do from the outer world. We know that our school is considered one of the best private schools in the east, academically, and that it has a waiting list. It is not social graces we are trained in but high academic and moral standards.

The headmaster, called Master Stanley, has all the correct attributes. He is firm and strict, yet kindly and just. He is a scholar, but at the same time a practical administrator. He is a leading Quaker and sits on the elevated front bench of the Meeting House, facing us all. He knows Nana well. She also sits on the front bench, but on the other side of the aisle where the women sit.

We from school, apart from the primary grades, attend Meeting every Thursday morning for three-quarters of an hour, walking over from the school buildings, across the grounds to the large square Meeting House, and filing in silently, beginning with the youngest, the boys on one side of the wooden aisle, the girls on the other. Between every four students there is a senior, or a teacher with the younger ones, to keep order. The temptation to create some form of diversion is always close to the surface during the long period of sitting perfectly still in complete silence. However, through the years, many students come to love this quiet hour, and to turn their thoughts quite seriously to contemplation and prayer.

Nana is almost always 'moved' to speak in Meeting and when she does we students wake up. She is always alive and colorful and what she says is related to our own lives. Some speakers drone on and on and we take no more notice of them than of the flies buzzing against the windows or the chirping of the sparrows under the eaves.

The Meeting House is quite large, very plain, without any adornment on its cream-colored walls. As you step inside you enter a hushed, silent world. The interior is a great oblong. The benches now have dark green cushions, but originally the hard wood was considered a more proper support for sinful flesh. On either side are rows of high, long windows, each covered with dark green venetian blinds.

Several of the older Quaker ladies still wear their bonnets to Meeting, tied with ribbons under the chin. Their dresses are gray or black. Nana broke away from such restrictions long ago and wears pretty hats trimmed with flowers or feathers. This has brought her quite a lot of disapproval, but she is such a pillar of the Meeting, such a popular speaker and has such a following, that the elders have not thought it wise to reprimand her too severely. At one point she was 'waited upon' and more or less given an ultimatum about her hats; but she said she thought the Lord didn't mind at all – in fact, He probably liked pretty hats and certainly liked people to look their best. Anyway, she was going to continue wearing them. So the matter was discreetly dropped.

I sit with my friends in the silent Meeting House. I have grown up in this atmosphere far removed from the busy world. As the minutes go by and everyone becomes more and more settled in their silent rows, the quietness seems to deepen. It brings a kind of balm to the restless soul. One is forced to stop and relax. Unfortunately, I have the kind of stomach that rumbles. When this happens, I am completely preoccupied with holding my breath, and avoiding the amused glances of my neighbors. Relief only comes when someone breaks the silence by getting up to speak.

November 1925 – Germantown

Life is picking up. This looks like being a busy social season. I have invitations to dances, dinners and theatre parties for several months ahead. A party of us have been to see Fred and Adele Astaire in *Lady be Good*.

Last night was Hallowe'en and we had a fancy dress dance at the Cricket Club. I had a wonderful time. More than that, much much more. I've had my first kiss. And from the handsomest boy in the class. He just danced me away, off the floor of the brightly-lit, crowded room onto the porch. It was a beautiful autumn night with a moon and everything. He took my hand and led me along the porch and then he kissed me, very gently, on the cheek. I was simultaneously astonished and transported. This is by far the most exciting thing that has ever happened to me.

January 1st, 1926 – Germantown

Another year has gone by already. I am painting my face with rouge and lipstick and I have let my hair grow again and sometimes put it up in a knot.

My bedroom is filled with pictures of movie stars.

I am also getting a crush on Byron. Byron, Keats and Shelley – I love the intensity of their poetry, the vivid images, the yearning.

I am full of yearning, but for what? A million things. What will the future hold? I am still safe in the familiar cocoon of my school. But there is not so much more time left.

Will I get married? That is the biggest question. I hardly dare hope. I have no self-confidence. I'm restless and almost driven. I throw myself into everything that comes along.

Just as I thought, my wonderful Stephen is now married. Not a beautiful young thing at all, but a rather plain, sensible woman. Why? I wonder. I meet them, but of course he knows nothing. He is always kind and teasing. My lips are sealed. I still adore him, but he will never know. I am no longer a little girl, but perhaps I seem foolish.

Then there is Charles, who kissed me that wonderful night. I meet him all the time, at school and at dances. We have a casual, friendly relationship but I see quickly enough that I am not the only one that he has so noticed, far from it!

The truth is that Charles is really interested in our class beauty; the rest of us are only for amusement. And yet, for a little while, I adored him. Who could help it? He is hand-some and fun-loving, really debonaire and he also drives a car.

The pain of life is something I begin to dread. It is agony. I become protective of myself and keep a guard over my feelings. There is so much pride involved.

Reading poetry – especially Keats – is a balm and an outlet.

'Heard melodies are sweet, but those unheard
Are sweeter. . . .'
Oh melancholy! A sweet pain.

There is a revolt in me against the commonplace, the routine and the obvious. Like Nana with her defiance of narrow customs, I strike out in my soul against dullness and meaninglessness. I hunger after I know not what – love, of course, but something else; not just love.

April 1926 – Germantown

We are all reading a book called *Kristinlavransdatter* by Sigrid Undset. I am gripped by it. I get very caught up in books. Above all, I am shocked and shaken by the detailed description of childbirth it gives. It fills me with dread and also with bitterness. I even begin to feel bitter against men in general, but not individually. I feel that I would dread giving birth to a child. I could not face the long drawn-out pain described in this book. As always, I am ashamed of my cowardice.

Maybe I won't get married. But if you don't get married you are a failure. From the very beginning a girl absorbs this fact. Everything in society is aimed at making it clear that you have to make the grade by being attractive. And yet, what can one do if one is not?

Warner has made a cat's whisker radio. It seems an absolute miracle to me. We listen to it with earphones. I can't get over being able to hear music this way. I have sheet music by the ton, and many records, but now I can listen to this marvelous radio. The best time is at night, after my brother has fallen asleep. I creep into his room, wrap myself in a quilt, and sit on the floor in the dark, the earphones over my ears, listening to all the dance music. It fills me with dreams.

July 1926 – Stockbridge, Mass

We have had our usual house parties and our two weeks at Eagles Mere. We no longer go to Whitford, after so many summers there. Instead, we visit Grandmother at her country house in Stockbridge, Massachusetts. It seems very tame to us, after Eagles Mere. There are mountains and pinetrees, but the air is not spicy and heady and the lake where we swim is muddy and dull. I am very bored.

In the house with us this summer is Grandmother's brother, a widower, much younger than herself, Walter Leighton Clark. He has retired from a successful business and is now taking up 'art' as a pastime. He is a strikingly handsome man, slim and elegant, dressed in gray tweeds. (He it is who, some years later, will found the Art Gallery on the top of Grand Central Station.) Since his wife's death, he has made his home in the National Arts Club in Gramercy Park, New York. As Grandmother is in fact our step-grandmother, he is no real relation of ours. We call him Cousin Walter.

He begins to take me around with him on his social calls with Grandmother's chauffeur driving us. One day we drive over to the studio of Daniel Chester French, the sculptor who did the statue of *The Minute Man* and, even more well-known, the figure of Lincoln in the Lincoln Memorial in Washington.

Mr. French is a slight gray-haired, gentle person. He seems very modest as he shows us around his large studio. He shows us first a small model of the famous Lincoln figure, about twelve inches high. He made this first, he explains. We then see a life-size model. We also see the molds from which his bronze figures are cast, many beautiful marble

38

heads, a lovely one of his daughter, a child's head. All his work has a charm about it.

Mr. French suddenly takes one of my hands and exclaims to my cousin about it. He asks if he may model my hands. This sounds interesting and we make an appointment.

*   *   *   *   *

We went to Mr. French's studio to have my hands modeled. It was so interesting. He worked very quickly. I put my hands down on a wooden work table. He covered one of them with a heap of wet plaster, then ran a string around each of my fingers, pressing it into the plaster. In a few minutes the plaster was as hard as rock. He then took one end of the string, and with great skill, pulled it bit by bit and as he did so the two halves of the plaster came apart as molds for the upper and lower parts of my hand. This was repeated for the left hand. He seemed pleased with the molds, holding them up and explaining how they would be filled with bronze and an exact copy of my hands would be the result.

*   *   *   *   *

Grandmother is getting really old now and seems stouter than ever. She is only one shape. Her dresses hang from her shoulders straight down to the floor. She is a great one for the social round and very correct. She is forever leaving cards on people, and receiving cards. She tries to get us to go with her, but we find such formalities boring, although we humor her from time to time.

We go to church in the village on Sunday morning and to the evening service held at a big house near Lenox. This is the service I prefer. We drive there just before sunset. The house is set in beautiful grounds and the garden has a view of blue mountains, the Berkshires, in the distance to the west. Several hundred folding chairs are set out on the grass surrounded by flowering borders. An altar has been set up facing the chairs, and the cross stands out against the sunset sky. The scent of phlox fills our nostrils, as we take our places and bend our heads in prayer. We sit listening to the chirping and twittering of the birds. The sun has almost gone.

Suddenly, in the distance behind us, we hear the minister's voice as he says the opening prayer, then the choir singing. It sounds far away in the late afternoon air. We hear the first lines of the opening hymn and the sound gets fuller and richer as the choir approaches, finally walking past our chairs, down the grassy aisle. It is an excellent choir, and as always, I am deeply moved by the beauty of the hymns.

The service is a short one. By the time the sun has slipped behind the high mountains and left a glory of rose and golden cloud, we have come to the final hymn. The scent of flowers seems stronger than ever – the air quieter. The choir walk down the aisle again, towards the back of the garden, singing. We hear the final Amen and then the minister's voice. We lean forward on our small chairs, our heads bowed. I pray silently, and seem to feel God in the garden, in the sky, streaked now with darkening clouds, and in the sweet flowers hemming us around.

Everyone stands up then and starts to talk, but I wish they would not do so. It breaks the spell. I wish we could have left with these other, more heavenly sounds still ringing in our ears.

September–October, 1927 – Germantown

My parents have decided that I am to go to college. This idea has been discussed for a good many years. I don't care very much. Some of my friends will be debs, a few will study. I will have to do something. I could have a coming-out party, but I really don't want to.

We have to face the fact that my school grades are not what they used to be. I have slipped. I am not interested in study – only in literature and writing. My parents had hoped I would go to Vassar or Bryn Mawr, but my grades are not good enough. They find a smaller college, Wheaton, near

Boston in Massachusetts. Wheaton will take me if I pass the college board examinations.

∗ ∗ ∗ ∗ ∗

We are all gossiping about one of the new boys who has come into our class this year. He is older than anyone in the school – twenty, we hear. We are impressed. He is quite handsome, blond and a good athlete – he plays on all the teams. He begins to come to some of our dances.

We went to a dance the other night held in one of the Boat House clubs on the Schuylkill River. My partner and I sat out quite a few dances on the balcony and amused ourselves by throwing a couple of wicker chairs into the river.

Another dance last night, also at a river club. The name of the new boy is Edward, called Teddy. He danced with me a lot. We finally went outside and sat in someone's car, an old Model T . . .

I am beginning to feel popular.

∗ ∗ ∗ ∗ ∗

We are seniors at last. For some of us this is our fourteenth consecutive year in this school. It has been my world, mostly a very happy one, certainly a privileged one, and even more certainly, a protected one.

The days fly by, packed with things to get through: examinations looming ahead in June, but also preparations for commencement, the year book to write, and so many dances, theater parties, concerts. I am caught up in a frenzy of activities.

'Soon it will all be over,' I think, but I find it quite impossible to imagine what the next phase will be like. I don't want to think about it. I'm not looking forward to college.

Besides, I am in love. It is more or less accepted by everyone that Teddy and I care for each other. He comes to see me every Sunday evening.

June 1928 – Germantown

I have left school on a high note of glory, fun and success at last. But now what? There is all the summer to while away, and then I leave home by myself for the first time ever.

Some of us are spending a few weeks at the beach, swimming and gossiping. We are waiting for our examination results. I have a feeling I will get through.

I am thinking of Teddy, who has taken a job in a hotel for the summer. He too is going to college.

I know Mother and Dad are not entirely happy about my relationship with Teddy. They are not sure that he comes from the right background for me. Their patronizing attitude makes me squirm, and makes me stubbornly defiant. I don't like superiority of any kind, and I won't tolerate implied criticism. I file away in my mind a silent reservation about my parents, a sadness and a disappointment. Why should some have privilege and others not? The question disturbs me deeply.

August 1928 – Germantown

The summer has almost gone – so quickly. It has been hot, and I have lived in my bathing suit. Nearly every morning there is a letter from Teddy lying on the floor beside the front door, and once I have this letter I am at peace. When he misses a few days, I am restless; has he met another girl? I am very jealous and doubt whether things will work out all right.

I know Teddy wants to marry me, but it will have to be a long way in the future. He has no money. Four years of college lie ahead of him. I have little idea what it takes to earn money. I have often heard Dad speak anxiously about money, even though he has a good law practice. As a family, we are extremely careful. Mother is thrifty and never goes beyond her house-keeping budget. In fact, she manages to save a few dollars every week which is put into the 'reserve.'

I have learnt all about this because Mother asked me to do the housekeeping this summer.

*　*　*　*　*

I've had my nineteenth birthday. Teddy came up to visit me. I'm busy packing my trunk for college. There aren't many days left. I'm beginning to get a sinking feeling whenever I think about it. I am afraid I will be too shy and awkward to find my way in a completely unknown world. What will the rules be and how will I find out? How will I know what to do when I arrive? It will be an ordeal to appear ignorant, and I will be too proud to ask.

I begin to feel cornered. Something is closing in on me. I remember the time I had that initiation. I was so stupid and so cowardly. Why am I this kind of person? I think about this a lot, but I don't say anything to my parents, nor to Teddy.

September 1928 – Germantown

My trunk has gone off and I am all packed and ready. Dad is going to take me to New York and put me on the train to Boston. From there I will be on my own.

Whenever I think of Mother and Dad, tears well up in my eyes and my throat gets tight. I wander around looking at all the places I love so much – the grape arbor, the wooden bench under the silver maple tree, the terrace garden, the three tall hemlocks and the fruit trees. Zinnias and chrysanthemums are growing in the garden, along with asters, marigolds, and a few phlox. There are some late summer roses in Mother's garden. A golden air is hanging over everything, with just a hint of what lies ahead when the leaves begin to fall and the bitter winds to blow. Now the bees are busy in the grape vines. Robins and blackbirds hop and run across the green lawn. A few butterflies flit silently from blossom to blossom. I think of Keats and murmur his verses.

This is home, and I am loved here.

II

DAD AND I had Pullman seats to New York, a situation which at any other time I would have enjoyed. But all too quickly we had arrived in the great rushing, noisy city, had taken a taxi across town to Grand Central Station, and Dad had placed me in the train, in a seat by the window. He kissed me goodbye, stepped out onto the platform, waved to me for a moment through the window, and then he was gone, having raised his hat and put it on again.

He can't have known what a miserable human being he was leaving in that train.

The journey went by quickly enough. Somehow I made my way at the Boston end to a waiting bus. Someone received us on arrival at the college campus. I followed the crowd, registered, and was shown to my room by an older student. It all went very smoothly.

My room is bare, square, rather dark, and directly at the head of the stairs. Two cots, two desks, two chests of drawers, a bare wooden floor – that's it. Sitting on one of the cots when I arrived was a pretty dark-haired girl – my room-mate. She was from New Jersey, and we hit it off right away. I did some unpacking and we went over to supper together.

*   *   *   *   *

Alas, the bell for the entire dormitory happens to be within a few feet of my pillow. This bell is forever ringing, summoning us to meals, to classes, to chapel. I hate it passionately.

45

That first morning I woke with a splitting headache and an aching body. Somehow I struggled into my clothes and went over to breakfast. My room-mate suggested I see a doctor. I did so, and was promptly put to bed in the infirmary. I had a temperature of 103.

* * * * *

I left the infirmary two days ago. I have missed learning the ropes; just my luck. But my room-mate has taken me in hand. I go to lectures and take notes but feel lost and bored. One class especially – zoology – completely mystifies me. It is worse than Greek to me. I'm sure I'll fail this course. I have made the hockey team though, and I enjoy the sense of well-being when we play a strenuous game. The New England air is gloriously sharp and clear and fills me with tremendous energy.

* * * * *

It is our second weekend here and lots of girls have gone away to Harvard or Brown's for football games followed by tea dances. I feel alone and lost. I have regular letters from Teddy, real love letters, but I would also like to be asked on a date. If only he were nearby.

October 1928 – Wheaton College

I have been here three weeks now, and at last I feel hopeful about what my college days could be. I was feeling very depressed and bored with the French, history and zoology classes, and then today attended my first English Lit. class. We were all sitting waiting when a young woman walked in and sat down at the lecturer's desk. We all stared. She looked younger than many of us. Was this really to be our professor? We saw a tall, not slim, young woman dressed in a navy skirt and blazer. Her white blouse was open at the neck and turned down over her collar, giving her a rather Byronic appearance, especially since her hair was cut very short, except for the front part, which kept falling over her eyes so that she had to shake her head and push it back again. She had bright blue eyes, pink cheeks, a small nose and mouth, which she kept twisting into an amused, quizzical expression. She was striking in her looks, but more than anything her face was lit with humor and intelligence.

I sat riveted through the lecture. She was explaining our course. We will be studying, among other things, Malory's *Morte d'Arthur*, a work I have not known before.

Her name, I have found out, is Eleanor Mackenzie.

I am, of course, in awe of her.

* * * * *

It is presidential election year and the campus has gone mad. I could hardly sleep at all last night because of the racket. The seniors have divided themselves up into Republicans and Democrats and are campaining vigorously all over the campus. The majority seem to be Republicans, since the shouts for Hoover drown out the feebler calls for Al Smith.

November 1928 – Wheaton College

Hoover has been elected and the country is settling down. Politics don't really interest me. Our family is straight Republican and always has been.

* * * * *

It is getting really cold here now. Most of the leaves have fallen, and we have had some snow flurries.

I have made quite a few friends. The letters still come regularly from Teddy, but I don't miss him the way I did during those first weeks.

The high point of the week is the English Lit. class. I have a passion for literature and for its writers, and our compelling young instructor has stirred this to a high pitch.

47

I have written several interpretive essays for her, and received them back marked with A's. So this is one thing I can do. She has asked me to read my essays to the class, and she has already told me, and some others, to call her Eleanor.

But the rest of college life is a bore, and I drift and dream and get by with as little work as I can.

December 1928 – Wheaton College

Today Eleanor invited me to come to her room for a cup of coffee. Only a few days remain before we all leave for home and the Christmas holidays. So the invitation was a very pleasant surprise.

When I knocked at the door she called out to come in. She was making coffee in the bathroom and told me to sit down. She was wearing her navy skirt and white blouse. The blue blazer lay on a chair. I have never seen her wear anything else.

I found it flattering to sit and drink coffee with her, as if she were an ordinary human being. I think she knows that I love the subject she teaches and that I respond eagerly to all she can give.

She began to tell me about herself. Besides teaching at Wheaton, she is studying for her M.A. at Wellesley College, which is nearby. She is very poor. Her father had a stroke five years ago and can no longer work, so she has been the sole support of her parents ever since she was sixteen. She is now twenty-one. She earned money working as a waitress in Schrafft's Restaurant while she was studying for her degree in philosophy at Wellesley. She told me what it is like to work in a restaurant when you are already dead tired at the beginning and have to be on your feet for hours.

I had never heard anything like it. I found it hard to take in – this charming young woman, only two years older than myself, struggling desperately to support herself and her parents.

She always has dark circles under her eyes.

I now understand why she wears her one costume day in and day out.

What kind of society makes such a desperate struggle necessary? When I think of my own comfortable, safe world and the even greater luxury some of my friends live in, I find myself getting very angry.

Christmas 1928 – Germantown

I travelled home in a train packed with students. There was no room to sit down, but I didn't mind. I was going home – having more or less won some modest spurs. Teddy was waiting for me, but I knew instantly that he was no longer the center of my world.

I'm not going to think about the future. Teddy is my escort to all the Christmas parties. He keeps trying to pin me down, but I avoid giving specific answers. I really don't know what I want. I feel oppressed by the way my parents and Teddy look at me, trying to find out what I am thinking.

January 1929 – Wheaton College

Back at college, and in a new room on the ground floor.

I have to face it; my life now revolves around Eleanor. And I am not the only one drawn to her. She is very popular with the girls. She is young enough to be one of us, yet is far beyond us in experience.

Philosophy was her major subject, and she is now trying to explain Hegel to us. I don't understand, and it all sounds more profound than anything I have yet grasped. But when she discusses poetry, I am really enthralled. She often reads to us from Malory and Keats and Shakespeare. Her voice is gentle, and casts a spell.

*   *   *   *   *

We have been asked to do a major paper for the end of term.

49

It can be on any subject. I have decided to do one on my faith.

February 1929 – Wheaton College

I have written my paper and turned it in. It is full of my favorite quotations from the Bible and from Keats. My vision of God blends and merges into visions of beauty. God dwells in the sublime fragments and snatches of beauty that come upon us unexpectedly. This beauty is balm and healing. It is also a restlessness and a hunger, a driving . . . My world is becoming more and more peopled with images, often unseen except with my inner eye, but deeply sensed and felt.

*   *   *   *   *

There is a place down in the woods, just off the campus, called Frank's Diner. It is off bounds, and forbidden, but we all go there. Many of the girls smoke down there, and I have learned to smoke, after making a fool of myself with the first cigarette.

The diner is warm inside, the windows all frosted up from the bitter New England cold. The coffee is delicious, the best I've ever had, and a large mug costs five cents.

I no longer miss my home and parents, no longer miss Teddy nor anything about my old life.

March 1929 – Wheaton College

My paper has come back with an A mark. That's pretty good. Eleanor was pleased. She read it aloud to the class. Then to my surprise she asked me if she could read it to other classes, and even more amazing, I have been invited to read it aloud one evening to a group of senior students.

I am pleased and flattered, and yet I can't believe the essay is *that* good. Why all the fuss?

*   *   *   *   *   *

I now go to visit Eleanor in her room quite often. She always seems glad to see me. She doesn't have much spare time though, as three times a week she has to drive her old Ford to Wellesley for classes.

Ever since my essay she has been talking to me about God. She doesn't believe there is a God. She gets out some of her philosophy books and shows me all kinds of diagrams and arguments that show He can't exist.

I was quite shocked at first. But she makes the point in such a profound and convincing way that I am beginning to wonder if she is right. When I am back in my room alone I feel a kind of panic about the thought of there not being a God – it's like having a house without a floor, you would just start falling, and never stop. It's a terrible thought; to even think it makes me feel a traitor.

But at the same time, it could be a relief. You could do anything. There would be no brakes . . .

*   *   *   *   *

Yesterday I went to see Eleanor. A voice other than hers answered my knock. I opened the door and saw two seniors making themselves at home. They were both wearing riding breeches and boots and must have just come in from a ride. There was something strange in the atmosphere. 'Eleanor will be back soon,' one of them said. She wore bright orange lipstick, which made her lips look greasy. Her face was a sallow almost yellow color.

I came slowly into the room, uncertain what to do.

'Come and join us in a drink. We have some very good wine here.'

I had never had to face this situation before. We never serve liquor at home, because my parents are afraid of what it can do to people. It is never served in any of my friends homes either, or at any of our parties and dances. I have grown up believing drink is evil and dangerous, and above all, that if I drank, I would be breaking a moral law.

So I was embarrassed when these two girls asked me to drink with them. There was something in their manner which was not friendly, a mockery that made my cheeks blush. They were definitely baiting me.

'Come on,' they said, laughing as they each took me by an arm. 'Come on, we'll have a good drink.' The sallow girl pulled a flask out of her breeches pocket and held it out to me.

I tried to push it away, but they wouldn't let me go. Finally, trying to think of an escape, I said, 'I can't drink out of a bottle. I'd need a glass . . .'

They roared with laughter.

'A glass? Ridiculous!' They each took a long swig from the flask, still holding firmly on to me. They were very strong and, as always, shame at my awkwardness kept me paralyzed, and I submitted rather than striking out. After passing the flask back and forth a few times they held me firmly between them, and, pushing the neck of the bottle between my lips, forced me to drink.

I was mortified; I felt that I was being forced to take the road to damnation and destruction.

Suddenly the door opened and Eleanor came into the room. She stared in astonishment at our three figures locked in this strange struggle. The two girls released me hastily, and then Eleanor really let fly. She was very angry indeed as she turned them out of the room. They went through the door, laughing together.

April–May 1929 – Wheaton College

My freshman year is drawing to a close.

I have been out on a couple of double dates the last two Sundays. I met a very good-looking boy from Harvard. We had a lot of fun.

*   *   *   *   *

I now go regularly to talk things over with Eleanor. She is trying to help me. She tells me she is an agnostic: the real world is totally different from what a person like myself

52

imagines• it to be. She treats me like a child, and this makes me feel as if I know nothing. I am also very jealous. She has become a security for me; her friendship now means more to me than anything else in my life. I know this is one-sided. I can see that I amuse her and exasperate her, yet call forth something protective from her. She seems to have taken on educating me.

*   *   *   *   *

Eleanor suggested that we should get away this weekend and take Peggy, a mutual friend, with us. She knew a cheap boarding house by the sea where we could sleep and swim and walk. 'I'm dead tired,' she said, sighing, and indeed she looked it.

So we three drove away this afternoon, all squeezed into the front seat of her ancient Ford. The seat was high and we sat looking down on the newer cars which hurried by us on the highway. Eleanor was in a cheerful mood. We all were. It was good to be heading away from the campus.

We found a small clean boarding house near the sea. We ate ravenously then lay in the sand. Eleanor slept. She seemed very happy, without a care in the world.

*   *   *   *   *

A threesome is not always the best arrangement, and by Friday evening I was getting into a bad mood. Something ugly and dark took hold of my will and kept me silent. Nothing had happened. I just felt jealous.

The other two enjoyed the weekend but for me it was a flop: worse than a flop. And it didn't help matters any when I realised that neither of my two friends had noticed my mood. They just ignored me.

*   *   *   *   *

Suddenly everyone is in a terrible state around here, and I

seem to be the cause of it. I can't understand why everyone is so excited and upset.

Last night, when we got back from our weekend away, I went to my room. I studied for about an hour, then got undressed and went to bed. Lights have to be out by 10.30. My bed is just under the window. As I was falling asleep I heard a scratching and tapping on the window-pane. There was Peggy's pale face looking in at me. I jumped out of bed and opened the window.

'Come on out,' she whispered. 'I've got two men here. They want to go for a drive.'

I didn't need any urging. I dressed quickly in the dark and went out into the corridor. No one was around. I unlocked the outside door easily enough and walked along the pavement. Peggy suddenly appeared out of the shadows and took my arm. 'This way,' she said, and we ran together down the path, across an open space and into the shadow of some trees. Soon we came upon the waiting car.

'Get in the back,' Peggy said. I obeyed, and found myself in the welcoming arms of Nick, my friend from Harvard. In a couple of minutes we were out of the grounds and tearing down the highway.

I was delighted to be away. My black mood began to evaporate. I felt a wild desire to escape from every confining influence, such as our meaningless college rules. I had been feeling bruised and confused.

We drove most of the night, stopping several times to get something to eat. Nick is attractive enough, but his cynicism and petulance stopped me taking him too seriously.

It was almost six o'clock and just beginning to get light when we returned to the campus. Peggy and I scuttled out of the car and made our way to our respective dormitories. I met several early risers as I walked boldly up the front path to my residence. One happened to be a professor going out for some exercise. I gaily said good morning. The front door was unlocked.

I was sleeping in my room when a message came to go and see the Dean immediately. I dressed and went to her office.

She was very upset and asked me many questions about how I had spent the night.

I told her straight out that I had left the dorm at 10.30 and returned early this morning. I told her how we drove around all night, stopping several times to eat.

She didn't seem to believe me and kept saying, 'Poor girl, poor girl.'

I didn't understand what she meant. I didn't feel sorry for myself at all. Nothing much had happened on our long drive. Certainly nothing serious.

I was then sent to the President. He told me that Peggy and I are to be suspended for six months. My parents are on their way to fetch me and take me home.

May–July 1929 – Germantown

And so I have left college, after only nine months. It hasn't turned out very well after all. I feel sorry for my parents. They are suffering – desperately worried and unhappy. They can't understand what has happened and neither can I.

I feel a fish out of water. I didn't want to go to college, and when I got there I found a world I had not been prepared to cope with. There are so many questions in my mind, but no one to talk them over with. At home it is assumed that we will always do the right thing. All my life I have known it is wicked and unthinkable to tell a lie. I have not told many – although I have kept silent about many things.

I have gradually accepted Eleanor's theory that it is extremely unlikely that there is a personal God. Therefore, all the fuss about right and wrong is unnecessary. I feel I can't tell my parents this conclusion, so we are living in two separate worlds.

Warner and Arthur, my two young brothers, look at me in wonder and curiosity. I have said nothing to them. I don't know what they have been told, if anything, about my sudden return.

Now it is almost June, I have six months to spend somehow.

*   *   *   *   *

I have met some of my old friends and been a bridesmaid at a wedding. Summer heat is upon us again. Teddy comes to see me every night. He has a job. I am glad to see him, but I know I can never marry him. He can't understand what has happened to me, and I can't explain it to him, although we discuss it endlessly. The world I grew up in has disappeared. I don't know at all what I really want. I think a lot about Eleanor and wish I could see her and talk. I am marking time.

* * * * *

I went on a picnic today with some of my old gang. We drove down to the beach and swam and cooked supper on a driftwood fire. But I already feel cut off from them. I keep wondering if they feel ashamed of me because I have been suspended from college. I find it hard to be natural with them, so I say rather wild things that I don't really mean, showing off my worst side.

* * * * *

I've decided to write a novel. The title is *Too Many Women*. I write every morning until lunchtime.

Mother and Dad have gone away and left me in charge of the house. My brothers are at home, and we are having a lazy time together. In the evenings I take my portable victrola out on the porch and play records. The music has such a haunting, evocative sound in the darkness, especially when there is a moon and the air is hot and still. Thousands of fireflies flit around the porch and are spread like a twinkling blanket across the lawn. They come and settle on my arms, turning their little lights off and on. As I lie in the hammock listening to the sad, sweet music, I dream and think and wonder. There must be something ahead.

August 22nd, 1929 – Germantown

I am twenty today. It has been a very quiet birthday. Teddy took me out to the movies.

My novel is coming along. I don't imagine it is any good but I enjoy writing it.

I've moved out of my bedroom on the second floor and taken over a large square room on the third floor with sloping eaves along one wall. It has four casement windows looking out westward over the Wissahickon Valley. I see the most gorgeous sunsets from the windows. I have put a table there where I do my writing.

October, 1929 – Germantown

The days go by. I am just waiting to go back to college. I have heard that Eleanor is not returning. She has moved her parents out of New York to a small house in the country, near Nyack. She has saved a little money and is going to try supporting herself by freelance writing. She has also started a 'library on wheels,' and has a daily route for miles around her home. Her letters say it is quite a success.

I hope she will be all right. Herbert Hoover is proving very unpopular. Times are hard and there is beginning to be a good deal of unemployment. I have never thought about such things before, but I can see that my father is anxious. So is Teddy. His brother is a stockbroker.

*　　*　　*　　*　　*

It is getting bitterly cold. We have our warm bright house and build a log fire every evening after dinner.

But I know not everyone is warm. Aunt Grace asked me to drive her this afternoon when she took sacks of coal to some of the poor families in Germantown. She and her husband, Bernard Waring, are active in the Quaker community. I went with her into the small, dark houses; the air was stale and damp. In our city of two million people, there are miles and miles of little houses, as cold and cheerless as those we visited. Aunt Grace gives real friendship to these helpless people. But I only feel a dull heaviness in my heart.

February 1930 – Wheaton College

I am back in college, in a nice room. There is deep snow everywhere.

I miss Eleanor but I have made several new friends. I'm still not at all interested in my studies and don't see the point of being at college. The Dean asked to see me, and we had a frank talk. I am not to leave the campus this term.

* * * * *

I have made great friends with an interesting girl, and we spend a lot of time together. She is a real rebel, tall and dark and strong. We have discovered a mutual love of music. She says she wants to go into Boston to hear the Boston Symphony Orchestra. Koussevitzky is the conductor and he, along with Toscanini and our own Leopold Stokowski, is tops. I feel I just have to go, yet I am forbidden to leave the campus.

My friend says they will never know if I slip away and don't sign out. We can spend the night at the Y.

I have no qualms.

* * * * *

The Symphony Hall was jammed but we managed to get two seats. It was a glorious concert. We were just leaving the hall, moving along in the closely packed crowd, when who should we meet face to face but our Dean. We merely stared at each other, exchanged no greeting. I knew the game was up.

* * * * *

I have been packing. Both the Dean and the President were very firm, and they have a right to be – I must seem a hopeless case and most unappreciative. I am glad to leave, though. It has been a waste of time and money. I am sorry for my parents, but I am defiant as well. I can feel my attitude hardening toward a lot of things.

March 1930 – Germantown

Now I really do feel completely cut off from the correct social world in which I was raised. I assume my old friends are fed up with me. I know from the way the family looks at me that I am a source of pain and worry.

I shut myself up in my room. I smoke heavily and struggle with my writing. I feel lost, but I dare not look too closely at my life. I mustn't panic.

Teddy still comes to see me every night. This passes some of the time, but we are beginning to quarrel. I can't make him understand what I don't understand myself, what has made me change. I only get impatient and irritated.

I feel such a deep dissatisfaction with everything – yet in a way I am not surprised. I don't think I ever expected things to work out for me. I just don't seem to be made for normal, ordinary living.

I *could* marry Teddy. My parents would support the idea, though not very enthusiastically. But it would be respectable enough, and that would be that. But I can't marry that way.

Of course I could get a job, but I don't want a job. I am too shy and proud to go around asking for one. And so, finally, my parents and I have decided I will go to business school and learn shorthand and typing.

July 1930 – Germantown

Business school passes the time and I rather enjoy it. I come home from the hot city, take a bath and sit out under the

trees. I am reading a lot: *The Seven Pillars of Wisdom* by
T E Lawrence, *Ends and Means* by Aldous Huxley and a
book by Sir James Jeans on the nature of the universe. I read
poetry. This poem of Byron's appeals to my mood:

> There's not a joy the world can give like that it takes
>   away,
> When the glow of early thought declines in feeling's dull
>   decay;
> 'Tis not on youth's smooth cheek the blush alone, which
>   fades so fast,
> But the tender bloom of heart is gone ere youth itself be
>   past.
>
> . . . . Then the mortal coldness of the soul like death itself
>   comes down;
> It cannot feel for others' woes, it dare not dream its
>   own.
>
> 'O could I feel as I have felt, – or be what I have been,
> Or weep as I could once have wept o'er many a vanished
>   scene.
> As springs in deserts found seem sweet, all brackish
>   though they be,
> So, midst the wither'd waste of life,
> those tears would flow to me.'

August 1930 – Germantown

Last night I finally ended it with Teddy. It was very painful
and emotional. He broke down and wept, begging me not
to leave him. But I could only feel pity for him and told him
firmly that he must no longer come to see me. Our affair has
now gone on for three years, and I am clear that I could
never marry him.

I am full of wild, proud, defiant feelings. When I feel
caught in anything, I strike out. I feel I am too young to be

put in the cage of a routine I can't control. It is quite something to be at once so fearful and so fierce.

January–May 1931 – Germantown

My parents have arranged for me to do some clerical work for one of the Relief Committees in the city. There is a lot of unemployment due to the Depression and quite severe suffering; there is also growing panic in the country. I work every day from nine till five.

The relief center is a huge ground-floor room, filled with rows of desks, in an empty building on South Broad Street. I sit at my desk, and one by one the people waiting around the walls of the room come forward to make their applications for relief.

I have to ask them questions and fill in simple forms: name, address, married or unmarried, age, number of children or dependents.

At first I was shocked at the number of women with children but no husband. They appear quite casual about it. Most of them shuffle forward listlessly.

I do my job rather mechanically. I am distressed by the whole sad, drab, tragic scene, the rather dirty, bare room, the harsh electric lighting, the smell. But I don't allow myself to look too closely or feel too much. I am locked in my prison of self-absorption; my own frustrations and bewilderments loom larger than the real tragedy of these helpless people. I am doing what my mother and relatives have always done – working for charity, giving a little of my time to help those 'less fortunate than ourselves,' a phrase I have grown up with. So many of the ladies of Philadelphia work for charity with hospital boards, orphan asylums, food kitchens. It seems perfectly natural to me, a part of life.

But it is with great relief that I step out into the fresh cold air of the winter streets at five o'clock every evening and pull my fur collar high up around my ears to keep out some of the bitter cold. I hurry to the suburban train, packed with commuters, and take my seat among the comfortable, prosperous businessmen and women. The car is warm and filled with smoke from cigars and cigarettes. We ride quickly out to our respective stations in the suburbs, away from that gray, silent, submissive crowd waiting so patiently for their small allowances of coal and groceries.

To open the front door of our house, step into the warm square hall and see the soft glow of the lamps shining on the walls; to smell a good dinner cooking; to eat it by candle-light before a log fire, seeing the beloved faces of the family around the table; to hear the bitter wind howling outside, the snow and sleet beating against the window panes . . . that makes me count my blessings in the most heartfelt fashion.

Later, when I slide between the sheets of my soft, warm bed and pull the quilt high over my head, I think of those acres and acres of cold, cheerless houses in the other part of the city. But no one ever says such contrasts are wrong – only one of life's harsh and unfortunate realities. I am almost guiltily grateful to be so comfortable.

*   *   *   *   *

There are now two other men who come to see me. One is a lifeguard I met at Eagles Mere. His attractions are not intellectual.

Then there's Harry, really good-looking, who takes me dancing.

I am dissatisfied and disturbed by the life I am leading. I know how shocked and distressed my parents would be if they knew what I was up to. I take care they don't find out. I don't want to hurt them – yet I have to have some kind of social life. At the same time, I know my conduct with these men falls short of what I would choose if I were able to meet someone I could really love and who would want to marry me.

I think it started when I got so emotionally involved with Eleanor and lost my love for Teddy. Any real meaning seems to have gone out of my life. I have lost an idealism I used to have. Now all I can see to do is to try to fill up my days with whatever comes along.

I have dropped all my former schoolfriends, so I don't have much choice. Most of them are married now.

I am in rebellion against the hopelessness of my situation. I get so bored with 'just going along.' Our home runs so smoothly. Everything is predictable – there are no surprises, not even in menus. It is very comfortable, but it can be stifling. I often wonder if our maids don't feel the same way – Mother is so orderly and precise. There is only one way, and that is the way Mother has worked out.

I told my parents that I would like to turn my bedroom into a 'studio' – with black woodwork instead of the boring cream paint there has always been. They have had it done for me. I have hung up orange curtains over the casement windows. The wallpaper is silvery ferns on white. There are many books and lamps and pictures, and the over-all effect is warm and glowing. This is what I long for, for the eye, for the spirit. It must be warm.

I have also installed a small cocktail bar.

I have plucked my eyebrows and wear lots of mascara as well as lipstick. I want to hide my face and feelings behind my heavy make-up. I have some spectacular earrings as well as an accordian cigarette-holder.

I try not to notice the expression of pain that comes over Mother's face when she sees me. Never was there a mother and daughter of such contrasting appearance. The other day when we were walking down the street together, some workmen whistled at me. Poor Mother, it was an outrage to her.

I have finished my second novel, but I have no idea what to do with it. I think it is better than the first one, maybe O.K.

June 1931 – Eagles Mere

I hear regularly from Eleanor, and she has sent me a subscription to a publication called *The New Masses*. Since it is a radical political sheet, I don't find it terribly interesting. She clearly wants to educate me along more revolutionary lines.

I have visited her twice in the home she has set up for her parents. She seems to just survive financially by running her library on wheels. I think she prefers the freedom of this rather precarious financial job to toiling away under more strenuous circumstances. She is also writing various articles.

I have long wished I could introduce her to the beauties of Eagles Mere and it has finally worked out.

*   *   *   *   *

We drove up yesterday. My uncle has given us the little cottage where Nana used to live. It is very simple – one large room with a stone fireplace and casement windows opening out on three different sides. It sits in tall, whispering, fragrant grasses, on the edge of the forest, but with a splendid view of the lake through the clearing in front. Like all the hotel's cottages, it is built of shingle, inside and out.

Eleanor adores it. I am so glad for her, and that I can give her a real rest with no responsibilities.

As so often in June, the weather is still quite cold, with a real snap in the air, especially at night and in the early morning. Soon after our arrival I telephoned to the hotel and asked for one of the bellboys to bring us some logs and make a fire.

In a few minutes he arrived. I stood by the fireplace and directed him, telling him where to put the wood and, when he had laid the fire, asking him to light it. He did it all pleasantly enough. He was a new boy, one I have not seen before. Each year the bellboys are recruited from the colleges and high schools and, although their wages are not high, they earn a lot of money in tips during the summer, usually enough to pay a good deal of their college expenses for the coming year.

No sooner had the boy disappeared out the door than Eleanor turned on me.

'How could you *ever* talk to another human being the

way you did just now?' she cried. 'It just made me boil. I was so ashamed of you.'

I stared at her completely bewildered.

'Your manner,' she said, 'the tone of your voice, the way you ordered him around, just a nice young boy who has to earn his living – so patronizing.'

'I had no idea,' I stammered. 'I certainly didn't mean anything wrong.'

She calmed down and now there was only a slight hint of exasperation in her tone.

'That's the worst of it,' she said. 'It's the appalling blindness, the unawareness of people like you, who've had it so easy . . .'

So easy, I thought. That's a new one.

We said no more about it, but the incident has sown a seed. I realize I have been used to giving orders to certain people.

*   *   *   *   *

The holiday went very well; we spent most of our time in a canoe or hiking through the woods. Eleanor responded through every pore to the beauty of Eagles Mere. How I wished I could do more, but the days passed all too quickly. She was very silent on the homeward drive.

July 1931 – Germantown

Nana has come to live with us. She has quite suddenly begun to look like an old lady, although her age is seventy-five. There has been much discussion about what should be done for her. She can no longer live alone, even with her maids to look after her. We have finally arranged that she should stay with us for part of the year, and with another daughter for the rest.

We find it strange and sad to see her so unlike the vivid personality we have always known. The light has gone out of her eyes and her countenance; her manner is dull and indifferent. She seems to have pulled a curtain down, and we are cut off from her. She is like a prisoner shut away in a silent world. It baffles me, and I cannot help wondering if she can still communicate with God. If she does, it is silently. She sits through the day in a rocking-chair by the window in her bedroom.

I still love her, even though I can get no response from her. I take her for a drive almost every afternoon.

I am living a quiet life. It is as if I am waiting for something to happen.

* * * * *

One hot summer afternoon recently I was feeling very bored, wandering from room to room, trying to get cool. There was a high pile of books on a table in the music room and I glanced at the titles, more or less indifferently. I have read most of the books in the house, though new ones are always arriving for birthdays and Christmas. Most tables in our house carry a pile of books and every room has an overflowing bookcase and sometimes two or three.

I picked up a large red book at random and began to read, sinking down in the nearest chair, and never stopping until four hours later, when the supper bell rang.

The book was *Dawn*, the autobiography of Theodore Dreiser. I went back to the book after supper and read all evening and late into the night, and through the next days whenever I was free.

What touched me and interested me in the book was the author's frank and honest admission of the things that had pained and shamed him – his awkward uncouth appearance, his embarrassment and suffering because he felt himself unacceptable, his hunger for beauty and for love, and his wonder at the world.

I seem to have found a kindred spirit, someone who has put down in writing all I have been bewildered by for so many years.

Dawn covers the author's life only until the age of nineteen. The notes say that Mr. Dreiser is now sixty, and world-famous, especially as the author of the best-selling novel, *An American Tragedy*. I have heard of him only vaguely.

*   *   *   *   *

The other day I drove Nana out. She wanted to look for something to read, so we stopped at a bookstore. While we were browsing, my eye lit on the name Dreiser. Sure enough, it was a cheap edition of *An American Tragedy*. I bought it instantly and, when Nana had made a purchase, we headed for home. I went to my room right away and started reading.

I get very caught up in a story, if it is a good one. This book gripped me immediately. Over the next days I read it straight through. When I had finished it, I slipped on my knees beside my bed, and wept. I was shaken by the tragedy of young Clyde on his lonely last journey to the electric chair; the tragedy, too, for the girl he had wanted to murder and who had drowned; the tragedy for the parents who lived in their own pious little world and never understood how things had gone so wrong; the tragedy for America, and for many Americans, whose aim was to rise to the top, regardless of the price to be paid. The book portrayed a young man caught in a system, driven by his craving to get some share of the spoils.

There was no one he could talk to, either, no one who cared enough to be a friend. Only at the end, while he was waiting on the death row of Sing-Sing, there was the priest, and then it was too late. Or was it?

I felt I had to express my feelings somehow, so I found a pencil and paper and wrote a letter to Mr. Dreiser, telling him how moved I was by this book and also by his own story in *Dawn*. I told him something about myself as well, my search for beauty and for a meaning to my life and how it has eluded me, and how lost I feel, and yet not too lost, since one always has the experience of beauty – books and music and nature, color and form, and of course dreams.

Describing all I felt to someone I thought might actually

67

understand brought me a sense of peace and ease. I put the letter away in my desk.

September–October 1931 – Germantown and New York

Cleaning out my desk today, I came across the letter I wrote to Mr. Dreiser in July. I read it through and was rather moved by it. I thought, why not send it to him, so I copied it out on my typewriter, addressed it to him care of his publishers, then walked down to the corner and mailed it.

In so many publications these days I notice Dreiser's name. He is much featured and highly praised in *The New Masses*.

*　*　*　*　*

As I came downstairs this morning I noticed the mail spread out as usual on the floor directly inside the door where the postman has dropped it. As I was sorting it, I came upon an envelope addressed to me in an unknown handwriting. It had a New York postmark. I opened it casually and saw, written across the top of the page, 'Theodore Dreiser.' The letter was handwritten. I started reading, my heart thumping with excitement: 'Clara, Clara – Intense, aesthetic, poetic, your letter speaks to me . . . from Philadelphia, where, once, for a time, I dwelt . . . would you come to see me here in New York, and we can talk? . . .'

I wanted to shout and cry out. What a wonderful surprise! This could be what I've been waiting for. Suddenly life seems marvelous. I feel on top of the world. Nothing matters now.

I've decided not to tell my parents – yet. I need time to think. I know I will go to New York. I will have to go. But not right away. This great development has dropped out of the sky, and it will unfold. I feel quite feverish with excitement.

I have just typed another letter to him. After supper I

68

will walk down to the corner and slip it into the mailbox. I have enclosed a photograph of myself.

* * * * *

Mr. Dreiser and I have been having a very intense exchange of letters over the last ten days. He wants me to come to see him. I am dying to go but I am playing for time. I am full of excitement, but fear too. What will it all mean? And what will my parents say and feel? I don't want to hurt them. I know they will be anxious. Mr. Dreiser's reputation – both as a radical writer and with women – is rather notorious.

He had already sent me two more of his books to read – *Sister Carrie* and *Jennie Gerhardt*. I love *Sister Carrie*. Once again, it is a story of people who are at the mercy of their passions and feelings and shows how someone can slip down to the very bottom of despair and degradation. His books show that Dreiser is a rebel against society. This appeals to me, but I know it will disturb my parents.

* * * * *

Today I received a letter from New York with a very different tone to it:

I asked you to be frank and you are, and frankness calls for frankness in reply. In some respects I like your estimate of yourself. It's at least definite and courageous.

Take this confession of yours: 'I guess I am in love with myself.' Well, then, you have never been in love. I have found beings whom I have loved more than myself and suffered for it. I cannot say that I regret the experience.

Again you say: 'I have always been loved and always expect to be.' There speaks the egocentric, self-centered to the danger point. Do you always expect to be loved? Such faith. For my part, I have by no means always been loved, and do not expect to be. Yet I have been loved too much, perhaps, or rather, more than I deserve. But loved too much or too little – how sad. Both involve something that is of the very tragedy of life. Of that – if I were to believe you entirely, you could know little. Your always expecting to be loved smacks of one who does not need or care to return love. To me – deadly dull.

You say: 'I do not lower myself for another but rather try to lift another to my heights.' Have you such immense heights to offer? As for myself, as of heights and depths I am dubious. There are only people for whom I would sacrifice much or nothing. They are heights to me or they are not. If they are – I seek, how eagerly, to find it.

Lastly you say: 'I fight to be alone. There are so many people always seeking, clinging.'

Fortunate soul. The security and very likely egotism of youth and beauty. But you may not always have to fight to be alone. The thought to me is humbling, for I have been alone much. Yet now the table has turned and I am not alone. Sometimes I must shield myself and garner my time, but for those to whom I must deny myself I am unutterably sad.

Lastly, so much of what you say indicates one who must be pursued and served. Alas, I am not one who vainly pursues or serves anyone. With love or a strong pulling, strengthening attachment, as you will, I will go hand in hand. As one of a rout attendant upon a beauty fighting to be alone, I would not endure – would not even set out upon the dusty pilgrimage. For it is not condescension that I am seeking, but a kindred, helpful, meaningful spirit. Your first letter seemed to indicate that you were such – or desired to be. These others, well – Yet perhaps at no time had you the intention to convey that. More than likely it is an ideal of my own that has betrayed me. But not too far. You must tell me more about yourself.

Theodore Dreiser

These words threw me into a panic. I realized I must make up my mind. I can't play with such a man.

And so I have told my parents about the letters and that Mr. Dreiser wants me to go to New York to meet him. He will put me up in a hotel.

They didn't know what to say. I could see they knew that it was useless to try to stop me.

I have sent a telegram announcing my arrival.

*   *   *   *   *

I feel unhappy about being so ruthless with my parents. If only I could explain to them how I really feel – why I know that nothing must stand in the way of this invitation. It seems an open door, the only door on the horizon, a door leading to life. It offers adventure and escape.

*   *   *   *   *

Today I went into town to buy some clothes for my visit to New York: a black fur jacket that looks like seal, but isn't, a black dress trimmed with red, a hat with a red feather. I have sent another telegram giving the hour of my arrival and received an answer telling me to go straight to the hotel and get a room.

*   *   *   *   *

I was close to tears when I kissed Mother and Dad goodbye yesterday morning. My small bag was packed. I had only to put on my hat and the fur jacket. I wondered anxiously what I really looked like. I was making a desperate effort to look worldly and sophisticated, but my hands were trembling as I lit a cigarette.

I was going in style; I had ordered a taxi and had a Pullman ticket from North Philadelphia. At the station I stood waiting for the long train to pull into the platform. A porter put me and my bag into my seat, and in a few minutes the train was moving again, silently, powerfully, smoothly, gradually picking up speed. I was launched on my great adventure.

It was warm and comfortable inside the Pullman car, nicely luxurious. My fellow passengers took their ease and so did I, gazing out the window.

There was much to think about. I went twice to the ladies' room to smoke a cigarette and stare at my face in the mirror. I was too nervous to read, or even to sit still.

Suddenly, in the distance, the towers of Manhattan sprang into sight, rising out of the ugly New Jersey swamps and flatlands. Then we were diving under the river and plunging into the long tunnel. I felt a pressure on my ears. It was a dramatic entrance to the great city – a roar, a rush, darkness, and then the smooth final glide into Pennsylvania Station. I tipped the porter and carried my suitcase to the escalator and along to the taxi cabs. People in New York seemed much more highly charged than the citizens of Philadelphia. I gave the address of the hotel to the taxi driver, and we were soon speeding up Broadway in the early evening light. It was already quite dark and the famous street was ablaze with lights.

I had never gone to a hotel alone before, and the simple process of checking in loomed as an ordeal in my over-active imagination. Would the clerk at the desk detect my nervousness and ignorance?

The clerk, who seemed frighteningly suave and worldly, watched me approach the reception desk. He shoved a pad and pen toward me and I somehow managed to write my name and home address. Yes, they had a single room with a bath! He snapped his fingers for a bell boy.

I rode up in the elevator and followed the boy down the long red-carpeted hall and into my dark, small room, comfortable enough and with the sound of New York seeping through the closed window – the roar of the sea of traffic that never rested, never ceased.

The boy did all the little things, turning on the lights, checking the bathroom, looking at the window, while I hunted for a tip. And then he was gone.

I stood for a moment. Now my heart really was

pounding. I looked in the mirror, my solemn image stared back at me, the heavy smear of lipstick, the hat with the red feather. I couldn't afford to think too much right now. My fierce determination to grasp this opening had got me this far. Now to see what would happen next.

I must pick up the telephone and ask for his room.

I managed to do this, and in a moment heard a man's voice saying hello. The voice was surprisingly high-pitched, in contrast to the rougher tone I would have expected from the large, burly image I had gained from his photographs.

I stammered out my name.

'Who?' came the rather querulous reply. He sounded annoyed.

I repeated my name and there was an abrupt change of tone.

'I'll be right down,' he said. 'What's your room number?'

I hung up the phone and for the first time began to relax. I lit a cigarette. The worst was over. I had no fears about meeting him. I already felt at ease with him as if I knew him. It was only the world that frightened me.

It seemed only a few seconds before there was a knock at the door. I opened it, and there stood a tall, large man with thick white hair. Once again, my impression was one of surprise – at the white hair. I had expected gray. He looked older than I had imagined, but otherwise he was exactly like the photographs. He came into the room, and I closed the door. We stood looking at each other, each drawing our silent conclusions. He was holding a rolled-up handkerchief in his hand. This too seemed slightly out of keeping with his somewhat rough exterior. He sat down in the room's only armchair. I sat opposite him on the edge of the bed.

'Take your hat off,' he said – his opening words.

I did so, quite obediently.

'That's better,' he said.

We talked about Philadelphia, where he had once lived and where one of his sisters had lived. While he talked, he rolled his handkerchief into accordion pleats and then shook it out again and started once more, pleating and rolling. I watched him, amused.

We talked easily. I felt completely at home with him. In my letters I had told him about my world, the world of books, music, poetry, dreams, longings. I knew we would never have to make conversation.

At first his looks gave me a bit of a shock, and yet at the same time I felt an attraction. There was a rough, massive force in the face, with its dark, leathery skin and the thick lips continually parted over the large, yellowy teeth. His eyes changed color, from green to gray to blue. He talked in a soft voice, in an almost gentle tone. I had found a fascinating friend.

And then his mood changed without any warning.

'Why did you come?' he demanded. 'Was it for the publicity?'

'Of course not,' I replied vehemently.

'I wonder,' he said. 'Many do, you know,' he went on, a note of cynicism coming into his voice.

I tried to explain what I felt about his books, especially about *Dawn*. It had been so reassuring to discover that there was someone else in the world who had had the anguish of struggling with a personality that seemed unable to fit into a normal, social framework. I felt such a misfit and I couldn't figure out *why*.

He mellowed and was very tender.

'You can thank God you're like that,' he said. 'It may be painful, but it's much more interesting. Most people conform like sheep and never have an original thought, and they are deadly dull.'

He suggested we go out to dinner, but first he must show me his apartment on the top floor of the hotel.

I put on my fur jacket again and took my hat in my hand. In a moment we were in the elevator, then stepping out on the fourteenth floor. When we arrived at his room he motioned me inside. I stood in an oval room, with three large French windows opening out onto iron-railed balconies. Along one wall of the room was a carved, wooden desk, a high-backed wooden armchair drawn up to it. Several large oil paintings hung on the walls. But it was sparsely furnished. Only the paintings belonged to him. The room was very neat. He told me that he worked at this desk sometimes, but he never knew where he would be doing his writing. Sometimes he wrote at his country place in Mt. Kisco, just outside New York, but more often he would have to go away somewhere; there were so many pressures, invitations, people wanting things. His voice took on an irritated, angry tone. He opened one of the windows onto the balcony and motioned me to come outside. We stood there silently, looking out over the vast city, now a maze of blazing and twinkling lights, with Broadway directly beneath us, winding its way in a shining cord the whole length of Manhattan. The roar of the traffic went on, but muffled now because of the height, with the taxi horns sounding more like bleeps.

Dreiser stood there, huge and stolid.

'My city,' he said. 'I have been all over the world, but this is home. I feel at peace here. It satisfies me.'

I could begin to glimpse what he meant, the power of the place, the vital, vibrant air. It was like plugging into a generator. It made your nerves tingle. The air pulsed with excitement. I could feel safe now, standing on a balcony looking down on it all, my guide and escort a man of the world. What a wonderful moment!

'Now for dinner,' Dreiser said. 'There is a small French restaurant where I often go. It is quiet and we can talk.'

We rolled along in the taxi, finally turning off Broadway onto a street in the mid-fifties.

I was amused at Dreiser's hat and said so. It was a dark gray velour, pinched together in three places to make a high peak. It was his own unique style and I could not imagine him in any of the more conventional shapes. He was wearing a blue shirt and bow tie.

The head waiter received us with pleasing recognition and deference and seated us in a corner of the small, softly lighted room. There were white table cloths and only a few other diners.

We had a seven-course dinner and a bottle of red wine,

and on and on we talked. We talked of Plato and Greek art, of astronomy, of Leonardo da Vinci, and we talked about Dreiser. He told me stories about his family, especially about his mother, whom he adored, and who suffered so much from poverty and all the terror that goes with it, being responsible, since her husband was incapable of holding a job, for finding the money to feed her eleven children. How Dreiser yearned over her and suffered for her and with her, and how he bitterly resented that life should use her so cruelly. He told me about his older brother Paul, the songwriter, who took the name of Dresser and wrote the popular songs *On the Banks of the Wabash* and *My Gal Sal*, and how he, Theodore, gauche and broke, used to seek him out and gaze in awe at the flashy world he moved in, the world of the theatre, of actresses and songwriters.

He told me about his marriage and what a bitter thing it had been; how his wife, being Catholic, would never give him a divorce, and about his recurring nightmare of being pursued by Mrs. D. wheeling a baby carriage!

He told me about his trip to Russia and about meeting Stalin, whom he admired very much. He said that Communism had, for the first time, set the ordinary man free from the hypocritical claims of the church and the stultifying bonds of marriage.

But, he said, it had not always been possible to get an adequate meal in Russia. Once he had bought himself some meat, made a fire in the snow and cooked his own meal over the coals.

Finally, the enchanted, leisurely evening came to an end. We were the last to leave the restaurant. Dreiser paid the bill and we walked out into the dark, quiet cross-town street. In a moment a taxi came by and drew up to the curb at Dreiser's signal, and soon we were back on Broadway with its dazzling, blinking myriad of lights, heading up town to 73rd Street and the hotel.

Upon arrival, Dreiser led me to the elevator, and when it stopped at my floor, stepped out with me and followed me down the corridor to my room. I unlocked the door and held out my hand, starting to thank him for the evening. He took my hand but came with me into the room and closed the door. I soon learned that he had no intention of leaving.

*   *   *   *   *

This morning we went down the street in search of breakfast, ending up at Horne and Hardart's Automat, where Dreiser introduced me to English muffins – such delicious food and so cheap! After breakfast we discussed my novel. He said he liked it. 'You write well,' he commented, 'but you don't say anything!' He went on disapprovingly about my lack of experience due to over-protection.

Then he told me about the book he is working on, *The Stoic*, the third volume of a trilogy on Charles Yerkes, the nineteenth century street railway magnate, who, along with Rockefeller, Morgan and Vanderbilt made and lost several vast fortunes. Yerkes even went to jail for misuse of funds, but finally clawed his way to the very top. Dreiser admired him, grudgingly, because he was clever and ruthless and aimed at the stars.

'I've just begun on the third volume,' Dreiser said. 'The scene is laid in London, where Yerkes was commissioned to build the underground.' Then he went on, 'I've been thinking you might be the one to help me.'

I kept silent, wondering exactly what he meant.

'I need someone to edit and prune my writing,' he said. 'I usually get help this way. I think you could probably do it. I'll give you a couple of chapters to try out.'

He went off then, saying he would meet me again in about an hour.

Left alone for the first time since my arrival yesterday, I lit up a cigarette, my thoughts spinning in a heady whirl. It had all happened so quickly, and in a way so naturally. In a few hours I had moved from being a complete stranger to this man, into a relationship of warm intimacy. I now had a powerful ally. In a way I was not even surprised – because of our correspondence. Our letters had verged on love letters, created on my side by the feeling I had for his books, on his

– I couldn't be sure – by my photograph, my own letters full of intensity and longing?

Where would it all lead? Then I remembered the question he had asked me; had I come for the publicity? I had been truly shocked at the suggestion and had hotly denied it. And yet, didn't I have to admit that the exciting element in this encounter was his fame?

When I had finished the cigarette I returned to the hotel and had only been in my room a few minutes when there was a knock at the door. I ran to open it and Dreiser handed me a large folder, along with a portable typewriter.

'It's in very rough form,' he said. 'Just see what you can do.' And then he was gone.

I went back into the room and sat down at the desk. The chapters were hand-written in pencil on plain white sheets of typewriting paper. I smiled to myself as I read. He did indeed need someone to straighten out his sentences which went on interminably, often for almost a whole page, broken by a series of semicolons, but rarely a full stop. The margins and spaces between the lines were filled with arrows and parentheses. He seemed unable to resist over-emphasizing and embellishing every point, as if afraid to omit any angle of interpretation.

I blue-pencilled almost every sentence, breaking down the long phrases into simple, comparatively straight-forward ones. I then typed it all up and, at lunchtime, handed it back to him.

He read it carefully.

'This is fine,' he said. 'Just what I want. Would you like a job?'

It was hard to take in all that was happening, but I quickly said yes.

*   *   *   *   *

When Dreiser put me on the train this afternoon, I sank back into my seat feeling a very different person from the trembling, anxious girl who arrived in New York forty-eight hours ago. Gone was insecurity and inferiority. I have found a wonderful friend and companion, almost a champion, who has vindicated what I have so often felt is the strangeness of my personality. I feel utterly at home with him. My preoccupations are his preoccupations. He is consumed with the same passionate quest – the search for meaning and fulfillment, the pursuit of the mystery of existence, a refusal to come to terms with the second-rate and mediocre and drab. And, to top it all, I have a job and a salary, doing work that can only be intensely interesting. I am confident that I can edit those long sentences.

I changed from the New York Express at North Philadelphia and hurried to catch the local train which would take me to Germantown. There was only one vacant seat in the crowded car. To my surprise I discovered I was sitting next to one of my old classmates from school. One of the 'bright' girls.

We exclaimed in mutual surprise. When I told her where I had just been she really did look interested. I felt the need to confide in someone, so we have arranged to meet tomorrow evening.

＊　＊　＊　＊　＊

I have been home a week now, moving through the days in a happy haze. When I told my parents about the job, they said nothing, though they could not hide their anxiety. I have closed my mind and heart firmly to any pain they may be feeling. It is sink or swim for me, a question of self-preservation.

Letters come frequently from Dreiser. My mother has agreed to go to New York with me to look for an apartment.

＊　＊　＊　＊　＊

Mother and I have been staying at the National Arts Club with Cousin Walter, while we look for a decent – and cheap – place for me to stay. We are so innocent and ignorant. We tramped the streets on the upper West Side, answering ads we found in the newspaper. Every door was opened by a slatternly, coarse woman. It finally dawned on us that we were in the Red Light district. My mother, a Quaker lady of the most impeccable character, has led an even more sheltered life than mine. We blushed together when a friend pointed out the facts.

At last we have found a room which seems passable; drab though it is, it is clean and the landlady is a decent type. It has one room, with an alcove for a kitchen and a tiny bathroom. The whole place is painted a horrible pea green. Under any other circumstances I would have turned it down as impossible. But I don't care so much now, with such an interesting life opening up, and so we have decided to take it.

November 1931 – New York

I have moved to New York and am settled into my room. I certainly didn't sleep much the first night. For one thing, I kept hearing a rattling noise in the kitchen. On inspection, it turned out to be a mouse. I was relieved and left him there, in a strange way glad to have his company.

In the morning there was no sign of the mouse. Breakfast was not as appetizing as some I have had. I boiled an egg, but there was nowhere to make toast. I drank lots of coffee. Outside, the great city roared and hummed. What a small gnat I felt, sitting in my ugly little room. What lay ahead, I wondered? Yet, for once, I didn't mind – the present was enough and was wonderful. And I had some hard work to do. I had been given four more chapters to edit and type.

About mid-morning, Dreiser telephoned and arranged for a period of dictation in his apartment.

We started work at eleven o'clock, he in a rocking-chair, his handkerchief in his hand. The pleating and shaking-out got underway. I had to smile – he made such an interesting picture sitting there, rocking and folding his handkerchief and frowning while he sought for words. He had worked out most of the chapters in advance and the dictation came smoothly enough.

*   *   *   *   *

For a famous novelist, Dreiser seems extremely humble about his writing, certainly not self-satisfied or vain. He often stops dictating to discuss a point he wants to make, testing it by my reactions. I say quickly enough what I feel, maybe too quickly, since I tend to be impatient of too much involved detail. However, he is magnificently firm and even stubborn about any point on which he has made up his mind. He is much more patient and thorough than I, and lets nothing turn him from his convictions. Any help I can give him is shallow, having to do with form rather than content.

He usually dictates for two or three hours in the morning. After lunch, which we take at the nearby automat, I return to my room, edit the story and then type it up. Meanwhile, he has returned the work from the day before. My neat, short sentences are now covered with darts, arrows, parentheses and long columns of handwriting down each of the margins. Once again I edit, retype and return. Once again he adds. And so it goes, back and forth, as often as five or six times, until he finally settles on a compromise. He takes the streamlining of his sentences with better grace than I take his refurbishing. We sometimes get into quite heated arguments on the subject, but of course I submit to his wishes in the end. I am discovering that it is very easy indeed to get my boss into a bad temper, and I am trying to steer clear of it most of the time.

Since his return from Russia, Dreiser has become an increasingly controversial figure, bluntly outspoken in his criticism of Wall Street, of big business, and of the Robber Barons. His sometimes savage criticism of the U.S. jars and irritates people.

*　　*　　*　　*　　*

The country is in a bad way. Mr. Hoover has not made the grade. He is bitterly attacked for the financial slump and the increasing unemployment. On every street corner, there are men selling apples – a scheme devised by someone in Washington as a respectable way for the unemployed to make a few pennies without actually begging. But everyone loathes it.

There is a good deal of talk about next year's election. They say that if Franklin Roosevelt is elected, he will actually do something. For one thing, he will repeal Prohibition.

But there is no problem for us about buying liquor. Dreiser makes his own. A gallon jug of apple jack, procured for him by a friend in up-state New York, stands in a corner of his apartment. He puts pieces of charcoal in it, to 'smooth' it. We drink a lot of this brew. It is pretty strong, but supposed to be comparatively pure. Bootleg liquor could have almost anything in it.

*   *   *   *   *

We go out to dinner every night, and every night Dreiser gives me more of his life story. I look forward to this so much after a hard day's slog at the manuscript. We are always more than ready for a drink.

Last night, we went to a speakeasy uptown in the mid-eighties. After our drinks we took the subway down to Lüchows, the famous German restaurant on 14th Street. Dreiser was quickly recognized by the waiters and led to a nice table. It was a large, warm, open, friendly place, abuzz with conversation, with the rattle of plates, with music from a string trio – all gaiety, bustle and movement. Dreiser loved the German food. We had delicious sausages and kraut.

There is more talk about his wife, who is still alive, though he never sees her, and some more talk about Russia. It is the coming country, he says. The people there are liberated from the bondage of fear and guilt that the capitalistic countries create in their citizens.

He told me how, at the age of fifteen, he resolved to defy his Catholic father, the Church – and God Himself – by refusing to go to confession. His father's failure to relate the principles of his religion to his relations with his wife and family had made Dreiser bitter and disillusioned. He felt his mother *lived* a Christian experience in her sacrificial care for her family, while his father only talked about it.

82

He told me how he sat in his seat that Sunday, when all the rest of the family went forward to take Communion. He was terrified: would God punish him? Nothing happend. He never went inside a church again.

He also told me about Helen, who is really a wife to him. She has been living with him for years, but since he cannot get a divorce, they are unable to marry. Helen lives at Mt. Kisco. She came, he says, one day to his studio in Hollywood. She was a young actress – nineteen. She rang the bell unannounced, and when he opened the door, explained that she had read his books and wanted to meet him. She was very beautiful, with reddish, golden hair. He asked her to come in. She did so, and he said, 'She has never left me since.'

Helen's life cannot be an easy one. Dreiser is not a man to be controlled or tied down, not even by a beautiful girl. There have been other women – like me – though Helen seems to be the only permanent one. He speaks of her tenderly and sadly. He knows he makes her unhappy, but he has no intention of being 'faithful.'

As for 'love' and marrige, marriage is out for him, but 'love' is very much in. He has come a long way from the awkward, gauche, self-conscious youth, yearning and mooning over any pretty girl. He still seems a little surprised, almost humble, at the way things have gone. He was a willing slave to passion, and even now appears to be still searching for the 'ideal' woman.

He is describing this search in his book on Yerkes, whose name in fiction is Cowperwood. In this last volume of the trilogy, Cowperwood, like Dreiser himself, after many storms and wounds, and slightly world-weary, is preparing for his final years. Cowperwood *has* found his ideal woman and has set her up as his mistress in a magnificent house in London. Money has bought privacy, a splendid art collection and independence from any annoying claims or demands.

Dreiser too is now quite wealthy, due to the sales of *An American Tragedy*, already translated into eight languages. Hollywood has paid handsomely for the movie rights to the book.

* * * * *

We walked through Washington Square on our way home from our dinner tonight. It was bitterly cold, with a cutting wind. As soon as we entered the Square, I noticed how many men there were stretched out on the park benches, some with a few sheets of newspapers pulled over their poor shoulders, many with no covering at all. I shivered, my heart stabbed to see them. Dreiser stood looking down at them.

'This is what has to change,' he said. 'This is the rotten fruit of a capitalistic society.'

'Is there nowhere for them to go?' I asked.

'The Bowery,' he said, 'but some would prefer to freeze to death in the clean air. Some of these may be dead by morning.'

Christmas 1931 – Germantown

I have been keeping in touch with Betty, the schoolfriend I met on the train last October. When I go home for a few days, I always look her up. She knows a speakeasy in Germantown, and we go there for drinks and long talks. She works in an advertising agency. I like her drawling voice, calm manner and philosophical attitude toward life. She is no beauty, but she has an inquiring, almost brilliant mind, and she's a very good listener. She has long reddish hair which she wears in braids in a really non-conformist way. She also has a nice sense of humor.

I am home for Christmas. Betty invited me to go with her last night to a party given by one of the men in her advertising agency. The address she gave me turned out to be just around the corner from my home.

A slender blond man in his thirties opened the door to us. He had a tall glass in his hand, and I heard ice cubes. This was our host, Mr. Anderson. His manner was easy, casual and friendly and I liked him at once. As we entered the living-room, his wife came toward us. She too with a tall glass. Though she was still in her early thirties, her hair had already turned gray, but was beautifully coiffed. She was smartly dressed, and a vivacious person who clearly enjoys life. They have no children, and Mrs. Anderson works in an insurance office.

They were wonderful hosts. Drinks were pressed on us, and it wasn't long before we were all in a joyous mood. Later in the evening, a young doctor named Bill joined us, bringing with him another young woman, followed later by interns from the hospital. In this one evening, I have made at least four very good friends. I have a feeling I am going to see a good deal of them. The Andersons' apartment is a perfect base for operations.

January 1st, 1932 – Germantown

Saw the New Year in with my new friends. January 1932. The party lasted until six a.m. I can't remember very well what happened; I can only remember talking all the time to myself. I wore a long red dress with gold 'brilliants' on it. I went to bed at home for two hours and then got up for breakfast. I am learning to do this, because there are many late nights now. If my family see me up for breakfast I think it will reassure them.

January 1932 – New York

Dreiser says he thinks we could find me a better apartment. He refuses to spend more than a few minutes in my little hole. He thinks I can get an unfurnished room for the same price, and we can dig up some furniture somewhere.

The winter is cold and bleak. The truth is, I get lonely when Dreiser goes to his country house at weekends, and I am too timid to go out much on my own. I usually eat my meals in the automat; I can't afford anything more expensive. Betty has come over for the weekend twice now. I take her to the speakeasy. For a moment when I knock on the door, I wonder if the eye which looks through the spy-hole will pass me. But he does.

We enjoy our drinks, which are pretty strong, and don't

care too much whether we eat or not. By now we are the closest friends. It is a real help to be able to say anything, and everything, to someone trustworthy.

The last time Betty came, we fell asleep rather late, in the double Murphy bed that lets down from the wall from behind a pair of glass doors. I was awakened suddenly by a sense of dread. Through the open window, I could hear the voice of a newsboy call a name over and over again. I struggled to catch what he was saying, but could never quite make it out. And then I fell asleep again.

We went out to have breakfast the next morning and bought a paper at the corner stand. I saw the headlines even before I paid for the paper. The name the newsboy had been shouting was Lindbergh. His baby had been kidnaped.

*   *   *   *   *

Dreiser invited George Jean Nathan, the drama critic, to join us for drinks last night in the club where we often go for cocktails. He is a rather small, slender man, with gray hair, dark, wise eyes, a small nose and wide, loose-lipped mouth. He and Dreiser are more or less buddies; that is, they get on together reasonably well, with allowances made on both sides, I am sure, for temperamental genius. They certainly are a contrast. Nathan is urbane and detached, smartly, smoothly dressed. He has a biting wit, as opposed to Dreiser's lumbering, heavy humor and smouldering reactions to events and personalities. But they united gleefully last night in their attacks on the American way of doing things, especially the hypocritical flaws of polite society. Society to them, or so they implied, is one big laugh. The world is run by lunatics. In fact, to listen to them, most people are lunatics.

Nathan brandished a long cigarette-holder. Dreiser never smokes. I brought out my own cigarette-holder. It was, I think, even longer than Nathan's.

We sat in a row at the bar and, thanks to a couple of cocktails, I was soon talking nonsense with my two companions. They reminisced about their great friend, the

86

journalist H.L. Mencken, agreeing that he was the limit; no one could hold a candle to him for wisdom and wit and a capacity to enjoy life. The conversation revealed an irreverent attitude toward all that most people take seriously in life. Listening to them, I found myself swayed by the force of their arguments, and tending to agree.

Dreiser has an amusing way of calling his men friends 'darling' when he is pleased with them. This word, in such a context, sits strangely on his lips, but there is a sort of naiveté behind it. There is certainly no sexual connotation. It has always been difficult for him to keep friends. He is so quick to suspect a motive or take offence. But last night he and Nathan were very chummy. They were discussing the possibility of editing a new literary magazine and wondering if Mencken could be tempted to join them. They also discussed the author and critic, Ernest Boyd, as another possible editor.

February 1932 – New York

Tonight, just as we were leaving a restaurant, we met Nathan coming in the door. It was quite dark in the entrance, but I could see that the woman holding his arm was beautiful. I saw a fur toque framing a white delicate face. A high fur collar was turned up around her throat and neck. She smiled at us as we went by.

'That was Lillian Gish,' Dreiser said, as we went out onto the street.

*   *   *   *   *

Dreiser has found me a better room, and I have furnished it very simply. It is a large square room, cream-painted (better to be bored then repelled), a kitchen alcove and a bath. The room has a fireplace, but I can't see that there is any chance of using it. It looks a little bare and sparse, but it is beautifully clean, with fresh paint. It is also six flights up, so I get plenty of exercise, since there is no elevator. So far, no mouse either.

Dreiser keeps giving me books to read. He is certainly determined to educate me. I have now read Dostoyevsky thoroughly: *The Idiot*, adored by T.D., *The Brothers Karamazov*, *Crime and Punishment*. Then Thomas Hardy, Somerset Maugham, especially *Of Human Bondage*, Zola's *Nana* and *Madame Bovary*, and John Cowper Powys. Powys appears to be Dreiser's most congenial male friend.

The searching poet in Dreiser's nature responds ardently to tenderness and sensitivity. His favorite adjective is 'aesthetic'; his favorite noun is 'sensuality'. If a person is both sensual and aesthetic, that person has something – is quite irresistible.

*　　*　　*　　*　　*

New York is now beautiful to me. When the wind is right, there is no city more sparkling with the sky such a deep, bright, cloudless blue, and all the towers and spires and walls of cement shining like silver, stabbing the sky. I am learning my way around by bus and subway. One can walk very easily for many blocks, which are much shorter, for instance, than those in Philadelphia, where they are called 'squares'.

When we go out to dinner and happen to start the meal with tomato soup, Dreiser carries out a little ceremony: he adds quite a large piece of butter to the soup and a spoonful of sugar, stirring it around until it is nicely blended. He also often goes into the smarter nightclubs armed with a bag of potato chips, since he is not at all partial to the nuts that are served with our drinks.

I feel sometimes that Dreiser is trying to place me in a category and can't quite do it. He is very interested in the kind of family I come from, and the social world I grew up in. He understands completely what happened at college, too, and states forcefully that I am better out of such an institution. It taught me nothing.

My protected upbringing often exasperates him, much as it does Eleanor. But he says there is hope for me because I am not a conformer, and have a restless spirit.

Theodore Dreiser, leading American novelist. I wrote to him in 1931, after reading his autobiography. He replied: 'Clara, Clara – intense, aesthetic, poetic, your letter speaks to me ... would you come to see me here in New York and we can talk?'

'The most amazing little 'gingerbread' house.'
Dreiser's home at Mt. Kisco, New York

With T.D. at Eagles Mere. 'He sat among my Quaker relatives, not quite at ease, I might say, really a little shy and sometimes not sure what to say.'

1935. 'My routine is well established now. I have at least two cocktails around five o'clock. After the drinks I feel peaceful and at ease. But I live in a bit of a self-centered haze, indifferent to my surroundings.'

Paris 1936. 'I miss male company. Nancy is kind, but boring.'

Mountain and forest vista near Eagles Mere, Pennsylvania

Aunt Marion. 'I looked up at her into
her very blue direct eyes. I didn't
want to lie to her.'

March–April 1932 – New York and New Mexico

Ernest Boyd often joins us for drinks and dinner now. He is more subdued and conventional than either Dreiser or Nathan, a solid man. Most of their conversation is quite beyond me, but I am content to sit among these three brilliant men just as a woman.

*   *   *   *   *

We were sitting at a table against the wall in a restaurant last night when a tall, thin, red-faced man with sandy hair walked into the room, straight up to the bar. He ordered a drink, gulped it down and was quickly gone again.

Dreiser sat very still, but I sensed his antagonism.

'That was Red Lewis,' he said. Lewis had never looked our way and Dreiser had made no move to greet him. He looked relieved after Lewis had gone.

He told me about his quarrel with Red, and that he felt Red should not have been awarded the Nobel Prize for literature in 1930. He told me how Red's wife, the journalist Dorothy Thompson, had arrived in Moscow while Dreiser was there. They met socially, though each was on a working assignment, and Dreiser said she made free use of the notes and information he had compiled about the Russian visit, and incorporated them in her own book, *The New Russia*. Then, at a banquet given for the Russian ambassador in New York, Lewis accused Dreiser publicly of having used his wife's material in his book. Whereupon Dreiser strode up to him and struck him across the face with his handkerchief! Friends separated them before things went any further, but any mention of Sinclair Lewis brings Dreiser to quite a boil!

*   *   *   *   *

The Stoic is going pretty well, but it will be a long book. Dreiser has done a lot of research on Yerkes' days in London and has his notes at hand when he dictates.

But there are interruptions, and he finds them irksome,

so he wants to get away from New York. He says we will go to San Antonio, New Mexico, a charming little place he has visited before. The weather should be lovely, much nicer than New York in February.

We are to take a boat to Galveston, with the car on board. From Galveston we will drive through Texas to New Mexico. I am to be the chauffeur.

* * * * *

The boat trip was short and uneventful, but when the car was unloaded at Galveston, I found myself in a harsh and rather threatening environment. I have never been West before, and the hot, flat, desert land was in sharp contrast to the lush green of Pennsylvania.

There was not a tree in sight – only from time to time the blowing tumbleweed and a naked-looking cactus tree.

On and on we drove – 300 miles at a stretch without a single sight of civilization. We had to be careful to fill up adequately whenever we came to a gas station.

But San Antonio is delightful. We settled in happily at a small hotel and got right to work.

The book is going well and we have made real progress. In the evenings we explore the charming restaurants in the town and drive out into the desert.

* * * * *

Soon, however, my boss got restless, and so we have moved on to El Paso, on the border of Mexico. Steady writing every day, but now at night we cross the border into Laredo and have Mexican meals. I don't like them very much, but T.D. does!

Last Saturday afternoon he decided he must take me to a bull fight in Laredo. I went along happily enough, enjoying the colorful spectacle from our seats in the stadium.

But when the first bull was let into the ring and stood shaking his head and looking around him in bewilderment, with the crowd roaring and cheering, my heart began to sink. The picadors rode into the arena and trotted around the bull, throwing their barbs into his neck until he was loaded with them. Then the matadors came on with their red capes and flung them before his eyes. I could see he was growing weaker and even more confused. He made desperate lunges at his tormentors, but when he was exhausted enough, one of the matadors went in with his long knife for the kill between the eyes.

Then such an uproar came from the crowd as the carcass was hauled around the dusty surface of the arena and finally dragged out through one of the gates. Dreiser informed me that the meat would be given to the poor.

But I had become violently pro-bull and anti-man. Three more bulls were killed that day, and then the crowd was satisfied.

Afterwards, we went to a café for a drink. As the barman handed me my cocktail, he reached behind him and picked up a bloodstained banderilla with its pink and yellow paper streamers. Smiling, he presented it to me. I took it and thanked him. It seemed the wisest thing to do under the circumstances.

May 1932 – New York

I have been brought up to care about appearances, far too much I am sure. I have defied this kind of conformity as much as I dare, but in certain circumstances I hate to be made conspicuous.

Dreiser and I have had a fierce quarrel, and it blew up so quickly.

We went to a small restaurant for a quick evening meal. We ordered omelets. They were a long time coming. When the platter finally arrived with its accompanying vegetables, I could see Dreiser beginning to tremble with anger. He began to swear loudly about having been forced to wait such a long time, and what's more, he said, on tasting the omelet, it was a lousy omelet, and the whole place was an insult. The waiter made great efforts to calm him down. He would make another omelet, etc., etc. But Dreiser got to his feet and said he could keep the blankety-blank place, omelet and all; he was leaving and never coming back.

I sat through it all with hotly flushed cheeks. Every eye in the room was watching us with amused fascination. Dreiser grabbed his hat and strode out, not even waiting for me. There was nothing to do but trot meekly and shamefacedly after him.

We were both moody in the taxi going home, but when we were back in his apartment, I let him have it. I was furious.

'All your talk about the poor downtrodden working man,' I said. 'You exploit them as much as anyone else. It's not consistent. That poor waiter was doing the best he could.'

We had a hot argument, but he wouldn't admit he had been unjust. The whole thing made me feel sad and disappointed. I consider this kind of inconsistency a flaw. It is one thing to write books about people who are exploited by a brutal system; it is another to live day by day alongside your fellow men in a spirit of toleration. But my points seemed to make no impression.

          *   *   *   *   *

Dreiser is excited because Sergei Eisenstein, the great Russian film director, is arriving in New York with his head cameraman, Tisse. We are taking them out to dinner tonight. I have never heard of Eisenstein, a fact which astonishes Dreiser; he once hoped Eisenstein would direct the film of *An American Tragedy*. Dreiser feels Eisenstein alone in all the world could have interpreted the book accurately, emphasizing its social significance as an indictment of the American system of free enterprise. Explaining this to me led him onto a favorite theme – cursing Hollywood for its rejection of everything except the familiar money-spinners: sex and murder.

          *   *   *   *   *

We met Eisenstein at the restaurant. He has a most striking head – large and domed, with the hairline half-way back. He is an affectionate and ebullient man. He and Dreiser embraced each other joyfully and uninhibitedly and settled down to talk and drink. Tisse was less demonstrative, blond and good-looking. He smiled and listened – perhaps he cannot speak much English.

The two big men were off into a world of their own. It was beyond me. I listened and drank my cocktails. At one point I tried to get into the conversation, expressing a rather superficial point of view, but Dreiser angrily told me to shut up. More and more rounds of drinks were consumed. We ordered and ate a meal, had more drinks and finally the two men called it a day. Everyone shook hands.

After they had gone, Dreiser turned on me;

'You don't know what you're doing putting in your two cents! Don't you realize he's one of the greatest artists in the world – and you have to push yourself forward. You understand nothing.'

He's quite right, I don't understand. I let him rave on. If I've annoyed or embarrassed him, that's too bad. I'll shrug it off.

*   *   *   *   *

Eisenstein has left town, but Dreiser keeps talking about him and about the great Russian experiment.

'I'm not a member of the Communist Party,' he says. 'They would like me to be, but I won't toe the line. I won't put myself under orders.'

However, I noticed the other day a cable on his desk with a Moscow dateline – an assignment to do an article for a magazine.

Dreiser is fighting hard for the cause of Tom Mooney, the labor radical who has been in prison for the last seventeen years under false evidence for the 1916 bombings in San Francisco. The other night, Dreiser asked me to go with him to a meeting where he was to speak on behalf of Tom Mooney. We took the subway to a hall uptown. It was a large dreary room, filled only with folding wooden chairs. I took a seat near the back. About a hundred people made up the audience.

Dreiser made his speech, but I felt uneasy and a little embarrassed for him. He is not at his best as a public speaker. He spoke in a strangely subdued tone. If only he had roared as he so often roars at me, in splendid rage and anger. He seemed another man.

There was mild applause when he finished, but many in the hall went up to him afterwards. His is a name to be reckoned with, and his support of Mooney is telling.

July 1932 – Germantown

Dreiser has moved out to his Mt. Kisco home for the summer. In New York I have no life apart from him, so I am spending more and more time in Philadelphia. I go to the Andersons' apartment – an ideal base for drinking, flirtations and lots of free talk with my friends. We enjoy being together and follow each other's adventures with keen interest.

The other evening the young doctor, Bill, entertained us with an account of a weekend he had just spent with some friends. These people had recently attended a meeting held by some people calling themselves 'The Oxford Group.' According to Bill, the Oxford Group's message is that you must confess your sins. We found this very funny – especially the word 'sin.'

July 1932 – Mount Kisco

Dreiser telegraphed me to come to Mt. Kisco, because he wants to get down to work again. I packed with some trepidation. What would Helen be like – and what would she think of me?

I stepped off the train this afternoon with my suitcase and stood looking up and down the platform, my old shyness turning my knees slightly weak. I saw a young woman with a white face framed with thick, long, reddish-gold hair. I knew it was Helen. She looked older than I had expected. But she is still lovely, though an air of sadness hangs around her. She seemed to recognize me as well, and we moved quickly towards each other and shook hands. I believe she was as shy as I was. She led me to her car, a smart blue Buick roadster.

On the drive to the house we made conversation, each trying to put the other at ease. I hate to be the cause of anyone's discomfiture, and Helen is someone who has suffered. She has paid a high price for her devotion to Theodore.

By and by we turned down a narrow lane and in a few moments the most amazing little 'gingerbread' house came into view, perched in the middle of an open, treeless lawn. As we drew closer, I saw that the effect is created by the bark shingles which cover the outside of the house. The front door and all the window frames are painted bright blue. Attached to one side of the dwelling is a passageway covered only by a roof. This leads to the guest-house.

Dreiser came out to greet us, and I was escorted to my room in the guest-house. It is small and rather dark and very simply furnished.

After unpacking, I wandered outside and found Dreiser waiting for me on the lawn. Several deck chairs were scattered about. It was a cool, fragrant summer evening.

I sat there, taking it all in. It is unlike any country house I have ever seen – something Dreiser has dreamed up.

We went over a plan of work for the next two or three weeks. We are really going to grind. We are still short of half-way through the book.

I am so glad to see him again. He seems mellow and contented, and pleased that Helen and I have hit it off – at least at this first meeting.

After a little while Helen appeared, accompanied by a huge Russian wolfhound. She was dressed in evening pyjamas. She brought a tray of drinks.

We went into dinner. The dining-room windows look out over the rolling green hills of Westchester county. I sat in the middle, between Dreiser and Helen, who were at either end of the table. The meal was served by a black maid.

After dinner, Dreiser took me downstairs to his studio – a long room stretching the length of the house. A row of windows occupies almost one whole wall, giving a magnificent view. On the opposite side of the room there is a large stone fireplace with easy chairs placed beside it. Down the middle of the room is a lovely refectory table. This is where Dreiser writes. The table was covered with books and stacks of handwritten sheets. He pointed out my small typewriting table in a far corner of the room. I am to have no distractions in the form of view or open fire.

I have retired to my room in the guest-house early, feeling not quite at ease. There is a tension in the air. This is not a home in the ordinary sense. Dreiser is a restless, seeking man, a driven man. Helen has dropped everything, given up her career as an actress, to follow him; just to love him. She is like the heroines in his books, but not like the heroine of the current book: Berenice Fleming, Cowperwood's mistress. Berenice has no intention of sacrificing anything. She loves, perhaps, but she expects payment in the form of acknowledgement of her power. She calls the tune.

Helen is ten years older than I; in her early thirties. Already Dreiser talks about her beauty as it used to be ... in ten years what will I be like? I won't think about it.

I never think about the future these days. The present is all-absorbing, but I know it can't go on for ever. I tell myself that something will happen ... I don't know what, but something. There must be something really *wonderful* somewhere. Perhaps some people die without finding a form of wonder or glory, but I don't want to miss out.

＊   ＊   ＊   ＊   ＊

Dreiser and I worked hard all day today and made some progress. I get bored when he struggles with the intricate financial angles of the plot: Cowperwood's buying and selling of stock, which he has researched in the London newspapers of the period. I know nothing about money. My father supplements the salary I receive from Dreiser, giving me everything I need. To be poor must be the most terrible thing in the world.

My father's voice takes on a certain tone when he tells us about his own father, the humiliation he suffered as a youth of fifteen when he had to go looking for a job, any kind of job, that would make him self-supporting, because my great-grandfather, a clergyman, could no longer afford to feed and clothe him. My father speaks of 'bitter' poverty, but I close the shutters of my mind against it.

But I find the romantic part of the Cowperwood's story more than interesting. I am fascinated by the qualities Dreiser writes into the character of Berenice Fleming. In Berenice he is creating a kind of superwoman, a perfect female being, a dream woman capable of satisfying the mature Cowperwood. Cowperwood is now a giant of finance and industry who is able to buy whatever he fancies – paintings, houses, lands, women. In a way he has bought Berenice, but she is the one thing he cannot control. She gives her love to the great man, but keeps her independence of spirit.

Dreiser must be putting himself in Cowperwood's shoes: he too has attained world renown after a struggle. He has known and loved many women. They pursue him still. I wonder who his Berenice is. Is she a reality, or is she a dream, someone he is still looking for? What does he feel toward me? Affection, I know. He wants to educate me, to enlighten me, even to help me learn enough about the world so I can write. We quarrel often enough, but he is mostly very tender with me. I seem to bring a certain tranquility into his stormy, contentious life.

I would like to be a Berenice, but doubt if I am!

* * * * *

Last evening Dreiser said it was time I learned how to make the best drink ever invented – a mint julep. We picked some fresh mint from the garden and carried it into his studio, where a bowl of cracked ice was waiting for us. I was set to work crushing the mint leaves in some sugar. When I had done enough, we spread this sticky concoction in the bottoms of two tall glasses and filled them to the brim with cracked ice. Dreiser opened a bottle of bourbon and poured it into each glass, also up to the top. The glasses were now beautifully frosted. He planted a sprig of mint in the top of each glass and we settled outselves in two of the comfortable chairs.

'You'll only need one of these to be completely happy,' he said.

We drank them slowly. They were delicious and, sure enough, in a few minutes we were utterly happy.

August 1932 – Mt. Kisco

We continue to work very hard. I don't see much of Helen. She is often out driving in her car and seems to have a life of her own with her own friends. She loves music and is often at the piano, playing and singing to herself.

But last evening was awkward. She came into the dining-room and took her place at the table. Dreiser was seated and so was I. As so often, they began on some domestic discussion. Then I noticed that Dreiser was working up into one of his rages. He shouted at her, but Helen revealed almost as much spirit as he and the room shook with the violence of their quarrel. It upset me very much. I have never before seen two people abandon all restraint and let fly with such passion. They were quite oblivious of me, and after a while I slipped away and went across to my room.

Today they were going on as if nothing had happened. I felt embarrassed for them last night, but realize now I need not have.

September 1932 – New York

So much has happened in the last month and I am still shaken by it all.

Not long after the evening of the quarrel, Dreiser

decided he needed a change of scenery. We went into New York for dinner and a show and, as usual, I had several drinks. Helen was to meet us later in the car and drive us back to Mt. Kisco. When she arrived, I offered to drive so she could get some rest. It was tedious going through upper Manhattan and along the crowded Saw Mill River Parkway. Helen sat beside me in the front seat, Dreiser in the back.

All went well until we got onto the Parkway. I had often driven there before but suddenly I found myself getting confused by the fast-moving lights. There were three lanes on each side of the dividing section and I decided to pass the car ahead of me on the outer lane. The stream of lights from the oncoming cars in the opposite lanes all seemed to be bearing down on me. I accelerated to pass the car and suddenly my wheels struck the wheels of the oncoming car. The impact swung us clear across the highway and we crashed into a wooden rail fence and plunged down a six-foot embankment, nose first.

I heard Helen screaming, 'My God, my eyes, my eyes.' I heard Dreiser groaning and swearing, and then almost immediately the whine of police motorcycles. Dreiser was out of the car and bending over Helen. She had been thrown against the dashboard and there was a cut over her eye which was bleeding heavily. Dreiser was shouting for a doctor and an ambulance. He seemed to be alright himself except for a large swelling bruise over his forehead, but he was terrified for Helen. In a few moments she was put into a car that someone had commandeered and driven off with Dreiser to the nearest hospital. I was left alone with the police. They questioned me and then drove me to the hospital. The car was wrecked.

I found Dreiser and Helen with her eye bandaged. Thank God there was no damage to the eye itself, only a cut and shock.

I felt like death. I was in disgrace. Finally someone offered to drive us the few remaining miles home. Dreiser was tremendously relieved that the accident had not been more serious. He was civil to me, but I knew he blamed me. Helen didn't speak to me.

*   *   *   *   *

A few days after the accident I was sitting alone on the lawn reading. A car drove up. A stranger got out and walked across the grass toward me. He asked if Mr. Dreiser was at home. I said no. He then asked who I was. I told him, and he said that he was from the insurance company and would I mind answering a few questions.

I fell right into the trap, as gullible and dense as anyone could be. He had a pleasing, smooth manner and led me on to describe just what had happened. I told him the truth as I saw it. When we had filled in the questionnaire's three sheets he held them out to me and said, 'Now, if you will just sign here.' I signed my name. 'And initial these other sheets.' I did as he requested. He stood up, put on his hat, thanked me and drove away.

It had all gone so smoothly that the whole incident passed out of my mind. It seemed perfectly natural to me that an insurance company would have to ask questions about what had happened.

Two days later the bomb dropped. Just before breakfast Dreiser rang me on the telephone.

'Come over to the studio immediately,' he said, and slammed down the receiver.

I couldn't imagine what had happened, but my heart was beginning to pound. It was clear he was furious.

The moment I entered the room Dreiser strode toward me, shaking his fist, his eyes blazing with wrath, his face flushed bright red.

'Get out of here,' he shouted. 'Get out of here immediately and never come back. You rat, you – !' He stood directly over me, tall and huge. I thought he was going to strike me. My legs began to weaken, but I was completely mystified.

'But what have I done?' I cried. 'Please tell me. I don't know . . .'

'You know well enough,' he said. 'Telling that insurance man all that stuff, and then signing your name all over the place. You've really fixed us now. You did the whole thing deliberately. Helen has often said she didn't trust you, and I wouldn't believe her. I thought you were different; that you wouldn't do mean things . . . but you're just like all the rest. Now get out.'

I began to see now that he thought I had tried to hurt Helen deliberately. 'I didn't mean to do anything,' I cried, stepping up close to him and pleading with him. But he pushed me away.

'Get out, get out,' he said and turned his back. I ran to the cottage, sobbing terribly. There I began packing my suitcase as quickly as I could, just throwing everything in any old way. I wanted to get away as quickly as possible. It was horrible, shocking, ghastly that Dreiser believed I had done this whole thing through jealousy and malice.

I telephoned for a taxi to take me to the train and when it came, drove sadly away. No one was around when I left.

I didn't arrive home until almost midnight. I took a taxi from the station and as it drove up our driveway and I saw the light burning beside the front door, waiting for me, I burst into a torrent of tears. I paid the driver and then stumbled up to the door, and pushing it open, flung myself into the arms of my parents, who had just heard me arrive.

'I've been fired,' I said. 'I've lost my job.' And I blurted out what had happened.

My beloved darlings tried to comfort me. What a solace they were when I needed them. This was the second time I had been sent home in disgrace. What a painful, confusing business life was . . . and this time the agonizing thing was that I was innocent of the motive imputed to me: innocent, but an ass and a fool; almost criminally ignorant of the ways of the world. That insurance man had made me do exactly what he wanted me to do.

I finally went up to my room and fell into bed. My mother knelt beside me and prayed for me. The sight of her kneeling there in all her purity and goodness of heart, made me weep all the more. How foul and wretched I was. I was breaking her heart – yet what could I do?

After she had gone I lay awake in the darkness. Sleep was impossible. It was anguish to think what had happened and to remember Dreiser's fury and his hatred of me.

I slept late the next morning. Just before lunch the front door bell rang. Mother brought me the familiar Western Union Telegraph envelope. I opened it, and read:

I CANNOT BELIEVE YOU WOULD BE DELIBER-
ATELY EVIL THOUGH I CAN'T UNDERSTAND
HOW ANYONE COULD BE SUCH A FOOL   COME
TO NEW YORK IMMEDIATELY.

Wild, delirious joy flooded over me. From the blackness of despair I was flung abruptly into the heights of bliss. He did, after all, believe in me. Even if I never saw him again, at least he did not think those evil things about me.

I packed my bags again, sent a telegram to say I would go to my apartment, looked up the trains, said goodbye to Mother. In less than two hours I was seated in the train heading for New York.

I had only been inside my apartment for a few minutes when the doorbell rang.

Dreiser walked into the room and stood looking at me, his hands on his hips.

'I can't understand anyone being such an ignoramus, such a dunce, such a fool, but somehow I have to believe you are innocent. We'll forget the whole thing.'

He told me that the affair was in the hands of his lawyer. I would have to see him, and Dreiser's insurance company, but things were not as bad as they might have been.

He said Helen's cuts were healing. She would be all right; there would be no scars. That is most important. But I can never go near Mt. Kisco again. We will have to work in New York.

November 1932 – New York

Franklin Roosevelt is now President of the U.S. and has inaugurated a New Deal to take care of unemployment and the country's sick economy. He is also repealing Prohibition, so we have moved from speakeasies to open night clubs.

I have a lot of work to do, and I am grateful to be able to slog at the typing, which has piled up.

I am developing the habit of taking a little drink, about eleven o'clock in the morning, just to relieve the monotony of the work. In my kitchen I have my own gallon jug of apple jack, into which I have duly put several pieces of charcoal. Until now I have held off alcohol until the evening. But now I keep thinking about this jug, so conveniently to hand, and so my daily intake is rising.

* * * * *

I don't see as much of my boss as I used to. We are still struggling with the book, but he is also giving me other things to work on – articles, also a collection of his poems, called *Moods*. I am planning to have my gang come over one weekend. Dreiser is to meet them.

February 1933 – New York

We had quite a weekend. I decided to welcome my guests with mint juleps in spite of its being a cold winter night. When Dreiser arrived, the three girls quite flung themselves at him. He adored them all. We forgot all about dinner until around midnight. There is only one bed, which we gave to the Andersons. The rest of us slept on the floor.

July 1933 – Germantown

I am home for a month. My parents and brothers are away, and so I am alone in the house except for the cook and two dogs. I am being very lazy.

I adore our rambling old house and the lawns outside, the tall, cool trees, the garden. It is so familiar, so pleasing to the senses. The heat dulls my mind. I lie in the hammock on the porch, listening to the summer sound of the locusts, reading, playing my victrola. The dogs lie outstretched on the wooden porch floor, panting and keeping a close watch on my every move. They are afraid that I, too, will disappear. They follow me all day long up and down stairs, from room to room, their claws scratching on the rugless floors.

I have met a man I like. He is a salesman. He is tall and thin, with light hair. His face is not handsome, but he has an off-hand, amused look which I like. He smokes cigars. One of my girl friends brought him along the other night and the three of us sat talking in the dark on the porch. I made some drinks. The fireflies winked and blinked around us. It was very hot and still. Our cigarettes glowed in the darkness, off and on like the fireflies.

I couldn't help flirting with this man. I'm sure my friend wasn't serious about him. She meets lots of men.

*   *   *   *   *

His name is Jim. He comes to see me quite often now, whenever business brings him to town. He picks me up in his car and we drive out into the country somewhere to get a drink. Sometimes we dance, sometimes just talk. He is something like Teddy, only tougher. His approach to life is direct and practical. He is bored with all the ideas we discuss when the gang is together. He has been married.

I know he likes me but I don't want to get involved. He is a good companion.

The summer days are going by very pleasantly. I hear often from Dreiser. He is at Mt. Kisco.

I am content just to be lazy in the heat. To read, to listen to music, to listen to the birds, to dream – to wonder at life, to know that in a few weeks I will be back in New York and at work again. I don't worry so much any more.

*   *   *   *   *

In the middle of the morning two days ago the doorbell rang. I went to the door and there once more was a Western Union Telegram. Now what? I read with amazement.

YOUR NOVEL COMPROMISE ACCEPTED FOR PUBLICATION $300 ADVANCE CONGRATU- LATIONS. T.D.

I ran around from room to room, laughing and exclaiming to myself. It was so exciting. I had almost forgotten about my novel, which Dreiser had placed in the hands of an agent.

Yesterday I had a long letter from him. He is very pleased and he, too, is surprised that my novel has been accepted so quickly by the first publisher tried. Indeed, he wrote, this shows that I can do even better. He suggests I hold the novel, not necessarily accept this offer which has come so easily, and aim to give the book more 'social' emphasis. After I have polished it, I can try one of the really first-class publishing houses; he says he will help me with the revision.

My spirits were slightly dampened by his letter. It would have been so nice just to go ahead and publish and receive a check for $300. But he is much more experienced than I. As he constantly points out, I lack judgement as far as the world is concerned.

And so I have agreed to do as he suggests, and all the joyful excitement has died away, like smoke or mist – dissolved in the atmosphere.

I know enough about writing to realize my novel is limited. It is a very slight thing, maybe facile, swift-moving, but that is all. It probably is unworthy of publication in its present form. Alas.

September 1933 – New York

I am working hard on Dreiser's poems. He is stuck again with *The Stoic* and looking for fresh inspiration. The poems show a different side of his nature – the side I respond to deeply. He loves all the innocent, gentle, helpless shades and moods of life, which he associates with wild flowers, birds, and the delicate tints of the sky. He is charmed by goodness and innocence and moved by helplessness. What he yearns for is unobtainable and almost indefinable, but in many of his poems he catches the fleeting moment, the shifting, haunting mood.

When we sit together and discuss these things I am happy. He is still the only person I know who is so deeply stirred by these mysterious intangibles, mirages which can seem more real than facts. The harsh, suspicious, contentious side of his nature is covered with a mantle of tenderness as he sits, huge and rough, describing in a gentle voice the wonder of a wild flower, of a bird song of piercing sweetness heard from a marsh, of the silent moon on a white winter night.

We beat our minds against the void – seeking, seeking, but no answer comes back. We stare in awe at the arrangement of existence, existence that never ceases to fascinate, to lure us onward, but eludes forever the clutching fingers of our minds.

We try to find an answer in music – Wagner, Beethoven, Mozart; but they, too, express only the same seeking struggle, the longing and the overcoming, perhaps, through submission to the way things are, but not the why or how.

*   *   *   *   *

Dreiser often discusses a book he has had in mind for many years. It is to be called *The Bulwark* and will be about a Quaker family. He is a strong admirer of the Quakers. He always seems to be searching for people who will not let him down, for an ideal that works, almost a form of religious utopia. Perhaps Quakers seem to him to be less hypocritical than other 'good' people. They do aim to practise what they preach. They are kind, unjudging, non-vindictive people.

I took him to Eagles Mere recently, and he sat among my Quaker relatives, not quite at ease, I might say, really a little shy, and sometimes not sure what to say. It was certainly a different world from our New York haunts.

He met my brother, Warner, and was captivated. Warner works for the Quakers and is a Quaker through and through – in bearing, manner and nature. 'He is a darling,' Dreiser said enthusiastically. I agree. One would trust Warner with anything. He is utterly dependable. His eyes are clear and guileless, his manner gentle. Sheer goodness shines from his face.

Dreiser has had little chance to meet people who live by a moral code, who do not tell lies or try to get the best of you. My parents would cut off their hands rather than cheat anyone. My father often talks about right and wrong, good people and bad people, but I only half-listen to him.

I don't tell my parents how I and my friends are living. It would be too much for them if they knew the truth. My friends come to the house to call and sit in the living-room with my parents. They all have good manners and know how to be charming.

January 1934 – Germantown

Thinking about New Year's Eve still makes me blush.

We met at a restaurant downtown for drinks. I was dressed informally in a pair of red slacks. We sat around a table together, all perfectly happy, everyone talking, but after many drinks I felt myself gradually losing contact with the conversation. Something was being decided, and I was being helped on with my coat and led outside to a large car, loaned by the Anderson parents for the occasion. I was pushed into the back seat along with three other people. It seemed we were going to somebody's house.

The drive went very slowly, in a rising snowstorm, with the windows all misted up, and a bedlam of conversation inside the car. Only the chauffeur stuck to his job and somehow managed to keep to the road.

We had been driving for almost an hour when I happened to look out of the window. The snow had about stopped, and I thought I recognized a familiar landscape in the moonlight that was escaping from the swiftly-blowing clouds. It looked like Whitford, and when we suddenly made a steep left turn down a road past a farmhouse, I knew it was indeed Whitford. I was shrieking out to my friends about where we were, but they paid no attention to me, naturally indifferent to my childhood associations. Then we stopped, and it *was* Meadow House. Stiff and cold, we got ourselves out of the car, all seven of us, and stood shivering on the stoop while someone rang the bell.

When our host opened the door, I was so full of my own memories that I walked right past his welcoming hand into the familiar hallway. A fire was burning in the great stone fireplace as we entered the living-room. I was in such a state of alcoholic and nostalgic confusion that I barely noticed our hostess and the other people sitting around the room. I could only think of one thing: the wonder of arriving here, so unexpectedly. How beautiful it looked.

I threw myself down on the floor in front of the fire, talking to myself. Somehow I took in the information that our host worked in the same advertising agency as Betty and Mr. Anderson. He and his family were now renting the house which once we had called our own.

At one point our host came and stood over me. I had the impression of a large, dark-haired man standing with a glass in his hand, looking down at me where I lay sprawled on his hearthrug. The faces and voices in the room became more and more blurred. I felt irritated at someone else taking over our old house, our special place. I resented the large man, whose face wore a rather set smile.

It was early morning when we finally left and stumbled out into the still cold air. Quite a lot more snow had fallen. It was very beautiful. I felt subdued and sad as we drove silently away. It had been a strange and haunting experience. Then I realized I had not said goodbye to either our host or hostess, and did not know their names.

*　　*　　*　　*　　*

I had lunch with Betty yesterday. We have found a little café in a narrow cobblestone alley between Market and Chestnut Street. These Philadelphia alleys are just as they were in the eighteenth century, with hitching posts all along them for tying up horses. They are too narrow for a car to enter.

We never have much money, any of us, and so we are always on the lookout for cheap places, and this one is very nice – a small room, with red and white checked cloths on the tables.

We ordered our drinks and Betty began to answer my questions about the people we met at Whitford the night before. Their name is Perrot; he is an Americanized Frenchman married to an American girl.

I could see Betty thought a good deal of him, and that it had meant a lot to her that he invited us all out there.

As she talked about him and praised him, I became more and more embarrassed. I couldn't remember anything clearly, but I did remember cutting everybody, and lying on the floor and talking to myself. It didn't make me feel any better when she told me what he had said about me: 'I like your friend but she has terrible manners.'

Thank heaven I will never have to meet him again and can forget all about it.

February 1934 – Philadelphia

I have lunch with Betty about once a week when I am over from New York. Yesterday we were talking intently in our small restaurant when Mr. Perrot suddenly appeared. He stood beside our table looking down at us. He has striking looks – a bold, large face with knowing, mocking dark brown eyes, a Roman nose, a thin-lipped mouth. His hair is black, and his large forehead is even more strongly emphasized by the fact that he is going bald.

'May I join you?' he asked, looking from one to the other of us.

My heart started pounding as he pulled out a chair and sat down between us. He put his elbows on the table and gazed with what must have been mock solemnity first at Betty and then at me.

'You mustn't be afraid,' he said to me suddenly. 'You needn't feel guilty because you made a fool of yourself. *I* didn't mind.'

I tried to explain about the house, but he brushed aside my tumbling words.

'Let's talk about something more important,' he said. 'But first of all I need a drink.' Then he and Betty settled down to office gossip.

I sat quietly, half-listening to them, but mostly absorbed in studying this unusual man. He had one of those utterly self-confident personalities, indifferent to opinion, individualistic. He seemed amused by Betty and me.

We finished our drinks and ate lunch, chatting away. I kept looking at his face. What lay behind those large dark eyes, gazing so blandly back at us? I sensed an ocean of experience. Inevitably I compared him to Dreiser. He was almost equally massive, but where Dreiser was transparent and obvious and sincere, this man appeared to mock, yet without bitterness. For Dreiser life was intense – a passionate, compelling experience; but my new friend seemed to accept everything with a shrug of the shoulders.

Whenever Betty and I commented or made a suggestion, he would say, 'Why not?'

After an hour Betty said she had to get back to the office. She stood up. Mr. Perrot remained seated, his elbows on the table.

'Goodbye,' she said. 'I'm late and have to run.'

'Of course,' he said. 'You mustn't be late.'

She was gone. We sat in silence. I lit a cigarette, but he didn't smoke.

'You have everything but self-confidence,' he said finally. 'A pity.'

I felt like crying and yet was warmed by his attention. He ordered us more drinks and then began to tell me about himself.

He was born in Paris, but at the age of sixteen signed on a ship bound for India. He was at sea for several years before he finally returned to France. In the war he was a pilot. Afterwards he came to America and married an American girl. He told me his wife is the perfect woman for him, and that they have three children. Now he is thoroughly tamed and domesticated in the American way. He writes advertising copy. 'What more could one ask?' he shrugged. 'It's surely a pinnacle?' All those dreams, those far-off lands. He spoke of his favorite city – Benares, the beauty and mystery and wonder of the East, and the poverty. Well, now he rides the commuter train every day.

The tone and the manner were intriguing. Was he telling the truth?

'But you,' he said, 'you are the important one. You are young. You can do anything.'

I was silent, looking down at my hands. A lump came in my throat. He said I could do anything . . . but what? What do I want? And even if I knew, how to attain it? I want fame and fortune. I want a wonderful husband. I want to be admired and loved. I want things I am quite sure I will never have. How could I describe my feeling of isolation to him?

He asked me about my work with Dreiser. 'Is he good to you?' he suddenly asked.

'Oh yes,' I said, 'he's good to me. He tries to help me get along.'

And I told him about my novel.

We sat until four o'clock, until we were the only ones left in the small room. I asked him several times if he wasn't due back at the office, but he only shrugged his shoulders. 'I want to talk to you,' he said, and that seemed to settle it.

But finally he admitted that he had to go. I left as well and rode thoughtfully out on the train. What an interesting man.

Spring 1934 – New York

I am working hard at my own novel as well as doing a good deal of routine typing for Dreiser. From time to time he tackles *The Stoic*, but it is sticky going. He tells me more about the Quaker book he longs to write – the story of a good man, who tries his best but is unable to help his children when they get into trouble. Dreiser says he has been much helped by meeting my family. He sounds almost in awe of 'goodness'; he admires the moral guts it takes to live straight. He would like to get down to writing this story, and yet he is hesitant. I think he may be afraid to tackle it because it is so close to his heart.

May 1934 – New York

I have finished revising my novel after a great deal of difficulty. Yesterday I dropped it in at the publishers Dreiser had chosen for me. The girl receptionist, sitting behind her counter, said nothing when I walked in, but indicated a large mail slot in the wall. I slipped the carefully wrapped brown paper parcel through and heard it land on the other side.

That was all. There was no one else in the office. The girl never stopped typing. One more manuscript. Who cares?

I have no real hope that I will receive another wonderful telegram. I am not really satisfied with my story. I think it may have lost some of the freshness and simplicity it had originally – even lost passion.

I've decided to put it out of my mind.

＊　　＊　　＊　　＊　　＊

I had a horrible experience two nights ago. I was sound asleep in my apartment when the telephone rang. I finally gathered enough consciousness to look at my watch. It was two a.m. I went to the phone and said hello.

A man's voice asked if I were Miss Clark. I said yes.

Did I come from Philadelphia?

Yes.

He then threatened me in a very coarse way. He said people knew what I was up to, and if I didn't clear out, they would tell my parents.

After a silence, I heard the click of a receiver being hung up.

I told Dreiser next day and he was quite worried.

'Someone's trying to blackmail you,' he said. 'There's lots of that in New York. You'd better get a chain for your door and never open it to anyone you don't know.'

'But who could it be?' I cried. 'I haven't done anything.'

'You don't need to have done anything. They just try to frighten you. Of course it might be something to do with the accident . . . It might even be Helen. She hates you now and often has too much to drink.'

His words have left me very depressed and uneasy. It is frightening to feel that Helen actually hates me. I wish I could make things up with her.

Today, on Dreiser's insistence, I asked the superintendent to put a chain on my door. He, too, agrees it is a wise thing to do.

June 1934 – New York

Last night about ten, I was alone in my apartment, reading and playing records. The doorbell rang. I looked up. The chain was on the door. What to do? The bell rang several times. I went to the door.

'Who is it?'

'A telegram,' a man's voice said. I opened the door, keeping the chain fastened. But it was not a telegraph messenger at all. The man standing there was not in uniform. I slammed the door shut and locked it.

Silence, and then I heard steps departing. I telephoned the superintendent. He said he would keep a closer watch, but there was no way of stopping people coming into the building.

August 1934 – Germantown

The publishers have sent word that they will not be able to publish my novel. So that is that. I'm not surprised, but I feel unenthusiastic about undertaking any more writing.

There have been no more threatening phone calls, and no more knocks at the door. Yet, something has changed. There are shadows.

T.D. is very busy, and quite often away. I have finished his book of poems.

August 1934 – New York

Dreiser came to see me yesterday. He sat himself in my one large armchair, took out his handkerchief and started folding and unfolding.

'The truth is,' he said, 'I don't think I can afford to keep you on full-time work here in New York any longer. I am between books now. I need perspective . . . I suggest you live in Philadelphia, come over for weekends and take work back with you to do at home. I want to give you some work, but as it turns up.'

It was a painful blow to hear these words and yet, at the same time, I feel almost as if I had been waiting to hear them. I was not surprised. Things haven't been quite the same since the accident, and I know well enough that his creative writing has reached an impasse. He has many preoccupations and distractions which I know nothing about – and all the pressures of being a world-famous writer. From things he has let drop, I realize he is beginning also to take the Communist Party more seriously.

'I hate to let you go,' he said. 'But why don't we try it on this new basis?'

We had dinner together. He was tender and mellow and talked about the goodness of my family, how rare people like that were, how evil and deceitful most of the world was, how I had helped him believe in something that he had not dared to hope existed, how I was an ignoramus and an ass due to my appalling ignorance and sheltered upbringing, but I must persevere in my writing . . .

Today I wrote home and explained the situation. I need to see how to move my few pieces of furniture back to Philadelphia.

114

September 1934 – Germantown

Warner worked it all out. The most practical of people, he offered to drive a truck to New York, pick me up with my things and drive me home in it. The truck belonged to the American Friends Service Committee, for whom he has done some work.

In less than two weeks I was all packed up and ready to go. Warner arrived early one morning. For fun, we set the chairs around the sides of the interior, and I seated myself in one of them, lit up a cigarette, opened a newspaper, and spent a comfortable two hours being driven home.

October 1934 – Germantown

I have worked out a simple and quite satisfactory existence. In the mornings I write. I have decided to write another book after all, and it is going well. In the afternoons I do any typing I have on hand from Dreiser, or else pass the time reading and listening to music.

Lunch is the worst time of the day. Mother and I eat alone. We have nothing to say to each other. I can't speak to her about my life, or what I am thinking. So we sit in silence. I try to get through the meal as quickly as possible. Mary waits on us and her comings and goings sound too loud in the silent dining-room. My mother concentrates on her meal. She has her own busy life of clubs and good works. My heart feels stony towards her. I am so bored.

Dinner in the evening is better. Dad is a great conversationalist and keeps a flow of interesting ideas going. I skip breakfast. I take a cup of black coffee and a cigarette after the others have finished.

I've already had one cigarette in bed, when I first wake up.

But every evening, once the family have moved into the living-room for coffee, I flee; I put on my coat, get the car out of the garage, and drive either to Betty's apartment or

115

to the Andersons'. We meet almost every evening. If it is Betty's, I take a bottle of gin, which we can share together.

Peter Perrot drops in from time to time. He never gives us warning, but suddenly there he is, large and solid, and amused. He is independent and elusive.

Spring and Summer 1935 – Germantown

The other night we all went to a hotel for cocktails. We were to meet a man there whom Betty had been asked to entertain – a travelling salesman, like Jim.

My drinking routine is well established now. I have at least two cocktails around five o'clock. After the drinks I feel peaceful and at ease. But I live in a self-centered haze, indifferent to my surroundings.

That evening I was sitting a little apart from the others, dreamily surveying the dimly-lit hotel bar. I watched Betty talking to her new friend. He was slight, with dark brown hair and a brown moustache. I vaguely noticed that he was looking at me across the room, but I sat quite contentedly, waiting for the moment when we would all move on to dinner. Betty brought him over to me and introduced me as Dreiser's secretary. His name was Richard Brookes. He was good-looking. His voice was cultured and warm in tone, with a southern accent. He said he came from Kentucky. I could feel a flirtation coming on!

*   *   *   *   *

I was called to the telephone about noon the next day. It was Richard Brookes. Would I meet him for cocktails at a certain hotel?

The cocktails continued on into dinner and a long evening. He was charming and flattering and for the next few days he quite swept me off my feet.

*   *   *   *   *

116

Richard and I have been deeply involved from the start. He is a cut above the normal salesman type. At first whenever he came to town, which was often, he would check into a hotel and I would go to see him there. Finally he decided to get his own apartment in Philadelphia and I helped him find one. He seems to have plenty of money to spend.

He is married but his marriage is on the rocks. He is a great martini man and we drink a lot when we are together. He is smoother than anyone I have met so far and I'm not sure I really trust him, but I like his attention.

Yesterday, a delivery van drove up to the house, with a large crate addressed to me. In great curiosity I got it open and found a large radio-victrola machine. I am thrilled with it. I can have some really first-class music. My parents are doubtful about whether I should accept such a gift, but I am determined to keep it.

Life has suddenly become hectic – seeing so much of Richard, going regularly to New York to be with Dreiser, and then there is Peter.

Peter has sent me a long poem – a love poem, really, which got me very stirred up. Another time he sent me some short stories he has written about India.

Whenever he drops in at Betty's he sits quietly drinking and looking at me, but I still don't know what he is really thinking. He has never made love to me – but he seems to be interested.

*   *   *   *   *

And so for the last few months I have been very busy. I go often to New York. One Monday afternoon I rushed back to Philadelphia to meet Richard and I bumped into Peter at the station. He removed his hat and stood looking rather sadly at me, bowing slightly, and saying nothing. I felt he knew exactly what I was up to, caught up in the excitement of rushing from one date to another. I couldn't say he disapproved, but I felt he might be disappointed.

Dreiser, too, seems to sense something. He had taken me to the station that day in a taxi. After I had bought my ticket, he stood with his hands in his pockets, the thumbs turned outward, his peaked hat perched straight on his head.

'You're different,' he said. 'Something is happening to you. But I knew I could never expect you to stay the same.'

I looked away from his eyes. I felt excited and defiant.

'Perhaps I am different,' I replied, and let it go at that.

The truth is I adore all these men, and want them to adore me. Each one is interesting, each so different, each so strong.

Loving people is a savage business, about the most ruthless and brutal there is. Dreiser used to talk about it; when a real passion once has its hooks in you, he would say, you are a goner – possessed, devoured, driven, obsessed. Creative work is impossible; concentration is impossible. There is only one thing to do – accept it and ride it out, like a storm, until it begins to wane, and so to lose its hold. Then normalcy gradually returns. Every fever eventually dies. And that is a sadness, too.

October 1935 – Germantown

I seem to have come to an impasse. There is a silly little development which I find worrying. My hand is beginning to shake, and it is embarrassing. I feel paralyzed even before I reach out for a glass, a cup, a fork or spoon. It is becoming an obsession – this fear of revealing to others what happens whenever I have to hold anything in my hands. Once I have had a couple of drinks, I am all right, but one can't always get a drink.

I am also beginning to wake up about four o'clock in the morning. I lie there and my thoughts begin to churn and tumble around. Fears creep in, like cold, clammy fog. What is really going to become of me? I am still young, twenty-five, but twenty years from now, what will I be like? I feel as if something were closing in on me, cornering me; something I have always half-suspected *might* happen – that I will miss out, be left behind, just fritter away.

March 1936 – New York and Germantown

I quite suddenly and unexpectedly received an invitation to spend some days with my Aunt Marion in New York. I was mildly surprised, but I accepted. It is something to do with my time.

I don't know this aunt as well as the others who live near us in Germantown. She is the youngest of my mother's four sisters. Living in New York has stamped her with a different air; a more worldly aura surrounds her, though when she is at family reunions she is completely one of us. She has a vivid personality and a great sense of humor. She is remarkably pretty: slender, blue-eyed, with thick brown hair. She dresses smartly as well. Her husband, too, is a charmer, a brilliant lawyer.

When I stepped into their apartment this evening I immediately sensed an atmosphere of beauty and taste. I was shown into a beautifully furnished guestroom, but it was the living-room which drew my deepest response. It is book-lined from floor to ceiling.

My uncle came home from his law office, and we had cocktails. Dinner was served on a drop-leaf mahogany table set against the bookshelves. We sat in the candlelight, talking. My hands shook as I lifted my glass and even when I tried to raise the fork to my lips. I was mortified. It was difficult to eat the delicious meal.

My aunt and uncle are so kind, so charming, so everything that I wish I were. I feel shabby, somehow, and shown up, though I know they love me. I was glad to escape to my room for an early night. My aunt says she will serve me breakfast at nine o'clock tomorrow, after my uncle has left for work.

*   *   *   *   *

I came out to breakfast at nine o'clock this morning in my dressing gown. I had already had my early morning cigarette and made up my face, adding plenty of lipstick.

My aunt was dressed and served me breakfast. She

looked beautiful, something like my mother, but more slender, and more volatile. She has a vibrant voice – very clear and bell-like, but also warm and tender. Like all the Warners, she has deep and passionate feelings.

And then the bomb fell. She suddenly asked me how many men I have slept with. I looked up at her, into her very blue, direct eyes. I didn't want to lie to her, so I admitted the truth.

I could see how much it was costing her to ask me this question; there were tears in her eyes. Then she told me that she brought me to New York because she could no longer bear to see my mother's suffering. 'Thee is a lost lamb,' she said.

I, too, felt close to tears, but my heart was hard. I just let her get on with it.

'Come into the bathroom,' she said suddenly. 'I want to try something.'

I followed her meekly and before I knew what was happening she had washed my face, taking off all the mascara, the eyebrow pencil, rouge, lipstick. Then she took a hairbrush and brushed my hair gently away from my face, trying out different styles and finally catching it in a tortoise-shell headband.

I stared back at my image in the mirror. I looked a different person.

'There,' she said, 'now thee is thy lovely self.'

She said they had some friends coming into dinner tonight and suggested I limit myself to two cocktails.

She took me around New York during the day. We had tea with some friends. I sat silently, tongue-tied, holding my teacup, afraid to raise it to my lips.

My aunt clearly wants to make a lady of me, but it is too late. Changing the surface isn't enough, there's something much deeper that's wrong with me. If anything, I feel more hopeless, because some of my protective shell has been chipped away and I am exposed. My aunt is a darling, but she has more on her hands than she realizes.

*   *   *   *   *

120

I returned to Philadelphia with my face washed and my hair brushed smoothly back under the band. My mother kissed me tenderly. She looked relieved, but we are still unable to talk together. I have given her only a vague, generalized account of my conversation with Aunt Marion.

*   *   *   *   *

Yesterday Mother asked me if I would like to take a trip to Europe. A friend of the family will be in London and Paris during the summer. Mother says I could make the crossing alone, and meet up with her there.

I have heard so much about Paris from my friends: rave descriptions of the French way – drinks at The Dome, café life. Why not go? I have no strong desire to see Europe, no sightseeing urge, but traveling should be interesting.

July 1936 – S.S. Statendam

Today was exciting and not a little frightening. Aunt Marion saw me onto the boat and helped me find my stateroom down on D Deck. Of course I am traveling tourist. I found quite a few bouquets awaiting me – one from Peter Perrot – and many cards and several telegrams.

My bunk is one of four, an upper one, quite close to the white-painted ceiling and away from the porthole.

Soon the gong sounded for all visitors to go ashore. I kissed my aunt. She quickly disappeared in the shuffling crowd. I pushed my way along the deck until I found an empty spot by the railing in the stern of the boat. We were facing west on the Hudson River, and the sun was dropping down the sky. The vast crowds were shouting, half lining the pier, half packed along the railings of the ship; the horns were letting out deep, vibrant blasts; confetti and streamers of colored paper were fluttering over us all. It was a magic moment when the propelers started up and we could see that the ship was very slowly moving away from the pier. I waved and waved, though I could see no face I recognized. Aunt Marion must have left.

How tight my throat was, taking in all this vivid, colorful scene, standing there at the rail, watching the pier slip further and further away, hearing the human voices become fainter and fainter, feeling the breeze from the river gradually strengthen and brush against my face. There was a long, golden path shining in the water behind us. I stood watching and watching: the gulls were screeching and swooping over the ship. I could smell the tarry ropes, the bilge and tangy, slightly damp air.

A man in a cloth cap came and stood beside me. He had a camera and was frantically snapping the skyline. Then a sudden breeze blew his cap right off his head. We both watched it sail through the air and fall into the swirling waters around the propeler. He turned to me and laughed. He was a German. We stood there talking together until the skyline had quite disappeared. It was already getting dark, and the evening star was shining on our starboard side.

Finally I went below to get ready for dinner.

My three cabin mates were busy unpacking. We all scrutinized one another but were not too interested. We didn't waste much time on conversation.

The stewardess had brought vases for my flowers. I stood turning the cards and telegrams over and over again. A sense of homesickness stole over me. Here I was, suddenly launched on a trip to Europe, almost in spite of myself. I had fallen in with the suggestion, but I couldn't say I was too enthusiastic. My life revolved intensely around a few people, and now this large, white ship was carrying me further and further away from everyone I knew and loved.

But I shut off a switch in my mind against these anxieties.

* * * * *

I love everything about being at sea – the throbbing of the engines, the long white-painted corridors and passages, the lounges, writing-room, bar, library. I went to bed last night, climbing up the ladder into my narrow bunk and sank into it gratefully. I was dead tired. I found the motion of the ship and even the slight rocking and rolling pleasing and soothing. I wondered if I would be seasick, but so far all is well. I may turn out to be a good sailor. My father loves the sea . . . my grandfather sailed around the Horn, lashed to the mast!

After breakfast this morning I wrote letters in the writing-room. It was a fine day, with a good stiff breeze and bright blue sky. There were so many possible choices as to how to spend the time that I suffered trying to decide between them. I wanted to be lazy and read a novel in the snug warmth of the library – and I equally wanted to read wrapped up in a steamer rug in a deck-chair. I wanted to stride around the deck and breathe the glorious salt air, and stand in the stern looking down on the churning waters left by the propeler. I wanted to sit and dream and gaze and feel and wonder. I wanted to play shuffleboard and deck tennis, cards, and sit in the bar with a cocktail.

And so I did all these things, one right after the other and the morning went by quickly. The bouillon at eleven o'clock tasted delicious. I was ravenously hungry.

So far I have found no one really cogenial on board. There are some young people who move together, but I am too shy to join them.

I went to the bar before dinner, limiting myself to the two drinks I promised my aunt.

*　*　*　*　*

It has turned out to be a smooth crossing. The sun has shone every day and we are now only two days out of Plymouth. A tender will meet us there and take off the passengers for England. We are due to arrive at five o'clock in the morning.

I have met a man from first class. It seems he stood looking down on us in the tourist section and noticed me and wanted to meet me. I'm not sure I believe him, but when he introduced himself and invited me for drinks in the first class bar, I accepted gladly enough. I have worked out a compromise on my vow whereby I only take two drinks at a time. This means two before dinner, two after, and I think I can make it two before lunch and two after. I can't really see why I need to limit my intake. It is important to enjoy myself on this special trip, after all.

My host was a somewhat red-faced older businessman. He wore a white dinner jacket and talked away. He invited me to stay for dinner. First class is ever so much more impressive and elegant than our crowded, noisy tourist quarters.

*　　*　　*　　*　　*

Everyone is preparing for the final night on board. It will be a big binge. I am all packed. In a few hours we will be in England, my first foreign country. Fortunately, Nancy James, our family friend, will be at the dock to meet me. I know this trip has been worked out in the hope that I will make a break from my wrongdoing. I know my parents and Marion hope against hope that something will happen to save me from myself. I know I am a problem and cause much heartache. But so far their hopes are unfounded.

August 1936 – London

We lined up in the corridors this morning to see the immigration officers who came aboard.

I had not been to bed at all. The damp early morning air felt cool and soothing, but the impact of arrival was somewhat dulled after so much celebrating. I followed the crowd mechanically, clambering aboard the tender. I looked across the gray water at England, and Plymouth, from which my ancestors had set sail almost 300 years ago.

As we docked, I scanned the faces of the waiting crowd. Sure enough, there was my guardian and chaperon in the form of Miss James. She was clearly excited and jumped up and down waving to me. I was relieved to see her and told her so as we fought our way through all the confusion of the pier in search of my modest luggage.

She steered me expertly through the formalities, brandishing large English coins as tips for the porters, who seemed extremely polite.

We struggled into the boat train, finding ourselves in a restaurant car laid up with white cloths and teacups. We dropped into two window seats, facing each other across a table laid for breakfast. Then two quite handsome Englishmen took the seats beside us. They were speaking together in loud thrilling Oxford accents. I was really in England! As the train started up and sped on its way up to London, Nancy and I exchanged smiles of pleasure in our splendid companions, who, however, paid not the slightest attention to us.

Nancy explained that she has taken a flat in an apartment hotel near Marble Arch. We will eat out, and 'do' London. She gave me some of the heavy English money to carry in my purse.

The flat is very nice, quite modern. It has a small kitchenette. I need a drink; my head is splitting. We have ordered two highballs from room service.

*　　*　　*　　*　　*

I am finding this first visit to England only mildly interesting. I miss my friends. If only I could have made the tour with one of them.

England makes me think of my father. Because of his deep reverence for the English law, the Inns of Court are like hallowed ground for me. So are the Houses of Parliament. He says that England has struggled for a thousand years to create and maintain representative government – and that, while far from flawless, it is the single most precious accomplishment on the face of the earth. Because of it, millions in the U.S.A. have had the privilege of life, liberty and the pursuit of happiness.

At the same time he feels England has been superior and high-handed with us during the last three centuries. The English have often treated us as an upstart, rather crude nation. Maybe we are. But I find the relationship one of interest. It draws out from me an intense, ardent Americanism.

Nancy and I go everywhere on the top decks of the big red buses, maps in hand. We have done the Tower of London, the picture galleries and Windsor Castle, but none of them were really exciting. And then today, as we stood outside Wellington Barracks, the Guards' band suddenly struck up, and a glorious wall of scarlet and gold and shining boots and towering bearskins passed by within a foot of my nose. I was quite unprepared for the glory of the martial music, the magnificence of the uniforms, the impact of the precision marching. Hypnotized, I joined the scarlet column, marching along beside them, prepared to follow wherever they would lead. Nancy marched with me, as indeed did many others. We only dropped away when the column entered the gates of Buckingham Palace.

*   *   *   *   *

English teas are marvelous! Nancy works as a companion-nurse to an elderly American lady, the aunt of Bill Tilden, the tennis champion. This afternoon she invited us to her hotel – cucumber sandwiches, scones and jam, buttered toast, lovely small iced cakes, and a trio playing popular dance tunes in the background.

I feel slightly guilty about Nancy. This trip to Europe is clearly a tremendous adventure for her. She loves sightseeing, studying the famous paintings in the galleries, reading up on the history of all the buildings, making the most of her time in England.

But I am not interested in sightseeing. I find it mildly amusing to be in a foreign land, but I'm aware that I'm very wrapped up in my own thoughts. I miss male company. Nancy is kind, but boring. However, if I have enough drinks during the day, life is more palatable and I am content to gaze at world-famous paintings, ancient buildings, historic cathedrals.

126

August 1936 – Paris

Yesterday morning we flew the channel from Croydon to Le Bourget.

Paris is bewildering. Friends have loaned us a flat on the Left Bank, just off the Rue du Bac. We managed to give the address to the taxi driver in our American French, but had more difficulty convincing the flats' concièrge that we were legitimate. She finally relented when we had produced enough letters.

The flat turned out to be on the sixth floor, and for quite a tip, the taxi driver carried up our bags.

We were both dead tired and wasted no time getting into bed. I was asleep instantly.

About five in the afternoon we woke up and discussed the possibility of food.

We found a small restaurant which we hoped would not be too expensive. There were rows of marble-topped tables; as we sat down at one of them, a rather fierce young woman, with frizzed dark hair, thrust two menus at us.

What to order? I couldn't understand a word of the menu, nor could Nancy. We thumbed through our dictionary, but even that wasn't much help.

The black-browed young woman hovered menacingly over us. She obviously felt we were idiots and resented our presence on her territory.

We solved the problem by pointing at random to three of the items on the card.

Alas, when they came there was not a hot dish among them – cold fish, cold ham, fresh fruit. We did manage to get some hot coffee.

We paid the bill which appeared promptly enough. She slammed down a white saucer with our change. There was a great variety of silver coins in the saucer and while I was studying them, wondering how much to leave for a tip, she swooped down on us once again and whisked the whole amount away, with a muttered 'Merci.'

Another long sleep. When I finally opened my eyes at noon, the sun was streaming in the open casement window by my bed. On the table beside me was a long French loaf and a bottle of white wine.

I sat up and had a lovely meal. The bread was delicious, and the wine washed it down very nicely.

Nancy appeared from one of her sightseeing forays and explained that she had gone out early and made this purchase all by herself. A great accomplishment.

But now we had to start looking for a meal again. How ridiculous to be hungry in Paris.

We went to an attractive sidewalk café and sat in the sun with our coffee. We finally managed to order ham and eggs – absolutely delicious! My vocabulary was returning.

*   *   *   *   *

We have now found a lovely café on the corner near our flat and go there every morning for coffee and croissants. I buy the *Herald Tribune* as well. The air is delicious, warm yet not hot. I love the smell of French cigarettes. I adore sitting on the sidewalk, smoking, drinking, reading, staring; what a superb way to live, and the weather smiles on. It is a caress.

*   *   *   *   *

For several days we have been doing the Louvre, Mona Lisa and all. But my thoughts turn to the childhood heroes who romped around these corridors and gardens and hurried along the cobblestone streets: D'Artignan, Richelieu, François Villon. I sit in the Tuilleries in the warm, quiet light, dreaming. I seem to hear their voices.

Paris is glorious. We are gradually becoming experienced tourists. I think I could spend my whole life in a sidewalk café.

Yesterday we made friends with two Frenchmen who were sitting directly behind us at the café. One of them asked us for a match, and when we smiled at them they came and joined us. They were very polite, and we each entered on a mild flirtation. Fortunately we didn't both fancy the same man. They have now attached themselves to us as guides and, most important, they know where to take us for a good meal.

They took us to an excellent Brasserie last night, where we had steaks and chips and a glorious green salad. I detected that they are not exactly wealthy, so we went 'dutch.' I suppose we appear to be rich Americans, but our travelers' checks are carefully rationed. Meals are our only expense.

*   *   *   *   *

We went to Versailles yesterday by bus, and today we packed. Tonight Nancy has flown back to London and I have taken the train to Boulogne to catch the boat back home.

Jacques, my friend, seemed distressed as he saw me off. He kissed my hand. I smiled at him but my thoughts were far away. I was melancholy and yet indifferent. He saw me up the steps of the wagon-lit. We stood looking at each other and then the sharp, surprisingly light, high-pitched train whistle blew, and we started to move. Jacques had given me a red rose and I waved it as the train gathered speed.

Of course I will never see him again. I know nothing about his private life, we have never discussed it. We lived entirely in the present, from day to day.

France seems beautiful and peaceful. I know nothing about what is going on in the rest of Europe. Politics don't interest me.

September 1936 – S.S. Veendam

This time I feel at home on board ship. Tourist class is jammed with students, and we had a noisy send-off.

The second day out we ran into a severe storm and gradually the lounges and decks emptied. I decided to stay in the fresh air and walk the deck, wondering if I could keep off seasickness.

I found a charming young American playing shuffle-board by himself. He had dark hair and looked mischievous,

129

yet cultured. I joined him and we finally ended up playing Russian Bank in the card room. We played it all day and half the night, endlessly, day after day.

He is returning to college in Minneapolis. I am quite smitten with him. We are having a wonderful time together. He is very American, fond of games and sport. Of course he is younger than I am. He is so different from the Frenchman, and from my friends in America. His name is Tommy.

*　　*　　*　　*　　*

Tommy and I spent the last night on board up on deck. I felt unworthy of him; shopworn, as if life has passed me by. If I had been less desperate, less fearful of ending up a failure, I might have met someone like him earlier, and he might have asked me to marry him. But I preferred self-destruction to rejection, and it is too late now.

The ship steamed up the harbor and I stood with all the crowd staring at the Statue of Liberty, but no emotion stirred in me at the sight of this famous symbol of my country's character. I felt dead inside, hopeless and indifferent. I was coming home – to what? To nothing I really cared about. I could see no future. I had had such high hopes, such inexpressible longings.

When we docked, everyone scrambled off the boat as quickly as possible. I saw Tommy in the distance but he didn't see me. I walked down the gangway, then saw my mother. We rushed towards each other. She looked wonderful – beautiful and tender. I felt like crying, but we set to work to track down my bags and get through the customs. Then Tommy came up. I introduced him to Mother.

'You mustn't disappear,' he said. 'I want your address.'

I wrote it out for him and he was gone.

Finally I was through with the customs and we were in a taxi heading for the train to Philadelphia.

III

Twenty-six years old and almost all my former schoolfriends are married. That's the rub.

I sit alone in my room at home, smoking and looking into the mirror, wondering what is to become of me.

My parents sent me to Europe to get away from bad influences. But after a day or two at sea, I threw all my resolutions overboard.

The trip wasn't really satisfying. The only real fun was with Tommy on that rough voyage home. His dark good looks and friendly personality drew me to him.

If I had any sense I would go out and look for a job. That's what most people would do in my place. But I feel too unsure and self-conscious for that – and this cowardice makes me ashamed.

I sit with my parents night after night, reading and playing solitaire. Tommy and I correspond. He's come to see me and we spent an affectionate day together in the country; and I've been to Princeton for a football match and lunch at his club. We are attracted to each other, but I'm not taking it too seriously. I'm playing safe.

*   *   *   *   *

Then suddenly everything changed.

*   *   *   *   *

Directly after breakfast some days ago, Mother appeared in the doorway of my room and asked if she could come in.

131

She sat down beside me. I could see she was struggling with herself, and this put me on my guard. Had she discovered something about the trip?

Then she blurted out that she was sorry for the way she had been towards me! She said that she had wanted me to reflect credit on her and had tried to impose her will on me. Maybe this was why I had wanted to get away from home.

She spoke with such love and sincerity – and her words were so unexpected – they pierced my heart. I broke into tears. We threw our arms around each other and both wept. In an instant we were united as we have never been before. All the love I really felt for her welled up in my heart.

Then she asked me several blunt questions about my relationships with Dreiser and my other men friends – and I told her the truth.

It seems that it is the Oxford Group – the people we laughed at so much at Betty's that evening in 1932 – which lies behind Mother's change of attitude. She met up with them on her annual visit to Grandmother at Stockbridge this year. She left me with a book about them: *For Sinners Only* by A. J. Russell. The title intrigued me and I started right into it.

The book tells the stories of people of all sorts who have faced the truth about themselves and found this the door to something new in their lives. As guidelines in doing this it suggests four absolute standards, taken from the Sermon on the Mount – honesty, purity, unselfishness and love. And it says that if people listen, God can speak to them, through their conscience and their best thoughts. The only block is what they call 'sin' – such an old-fashioned word.

I feel stirred up and excited. At the darkest point five years ago, a book showed me the way to adventure, through meeting Dreiser. Maybe it will be the same with this book – and the others Mother has lent me. All at once I have plenty to think about.

*   *   *   *   *

Yesterday, two weeks after my talk with Mother, I went out

into the garden alone. I sat quietly in the deck-chair under the trees in the stillness of a beautiful autumn day. The warm sunshine beat down on my head. It felt like a benediction. It was so still – only a few leaves dropping, one by one, at intervals. I thought of the leaves falling in the last scene of *Cyrano de Bergerac:* all had become clear then, misunderstandings put right.

I prayed.

And all at once a clear thought came into my mind.

'Admit you are a failure.'

My heart constricted, yet I knew this was the cold, hard reality. I wrote the thought down, so as to remember it.

Then: 'You are whistling in the dark. Stop running away. You are ashamed because you are not married.'

I could feel my cheeks flushing as I looked at what I had written. I sat quiet for a long time, just living with the truth I had faced head on.

＊　＊　＊　＊　＊

The more I read about these people who have found an answer in their lives, the surer I feel that I have somehow been led to a way out. I remember the days of my childhood when God seemed so real to me. I never doubted his existence then. When Eleanor began to argue against the possibility of his existence it was such a shock. But then after college I flung away all the safeguards and took off the brakes, and my sense of right and wrong gradually died.

Quite early on I was able to rationalise the things I wanted to do. I can remember hovering over my mother's jewelry box and trying on the different pieces. Several of them found their way into my bureau drawer. Much more recently I found three jeweled stick-pins in my father's case, which had gone out of fashion and he no longer wore. I gave one of them to Peter, who seemed very pleased with it.

I never took money, but these other thefts never bothered my conscience until now.

I have to confess that the only one of those absolute

standards which makes any sense to me is honesty. I don't understand what is meant by 'absolute purity.'

I have started reading the Bible again – and find myself seeing it through new eyes.

*   *   *   *   *

Yesterday one of the people described in *For Sinners Only* arrived at our house. His name was Cleve Hicks. It was to him that Mother unburdened herself in Stockbridge. We all greeted him at the front door. Having now read so much about the Oxford Group, I was intensely curious to see what this first flesh and blood representative would be like.

He surprised me. He was a large man with a round face and merry blue eyes, bubbling over with joie de vivre, the sort of person who enlivens the atmosphere of a house as soon as he enters. Yet later, at dinner, he embarked on a serious discussion of world affairs.

There was a point of interest in his name. My father drew from him that he is a descendant of Elias Hicks, who founded the Hicksite branch of the Quakers. In spite of this, however, Mr. Hicks turns out to be the son of an Episcopalian bishop! After dinner Dad asked our guest if he would select a passage from the Bible for our evening reading.

Mr Hicks turned to me and asked if I would choose something.

I thought quickly, eager to show off my newly-revived religious knowledge. I settled on John XIV. The language is so supremely beautiful, and it presents God as a loving father – for me, a wayward child.

'Would you like to read it to us?' he asked.

And so I read the whole chapter, grateful to him for including me.

Before he left today, he invited Mother and me to spend a weekend at the Group headquarters in New York. He said there would be many people of my age there.

October 1936 – New York

This morning I put on plenty of lipstick and packed a small suitcase. Off to New York again, but with what a different purpose! Mother looked at my war-paint and suggested I tone it down a bit. She has been telling me recently how often she used to feel ashamed to walk down the street with me and hear the cat-calls and whistles.

Our instructions were to go first to the Gramercy Park Hotel, where a room was reserved for us, and then to make our way to 61 Gramercy Park, just one block away.

This is familiar territory to me since my visits to Cousin Walter Clark at the National Arts Club, also on the square. Behind its tall black iron fence and bordered by old brownstone houses, the park is a haven in the hurly-burly of New York. It has wooden benches, a patch of grass and carefully tended flower beds. Residents on the square have keys to a private entrance.

As we made our way down the street to Number 61, I was thinking of my old New York friends, somewhere in the vast city, probably just setting off for evening cocktails. If only they could have seen me!

61 Gramercy Park turned out to be a tall red-brick building attached to Calvary Church. The rector, the Rev. Samuel Shoemaker, has given over his church building for use as the headquarters of the Oxford Group in America.

We rang the bell and were welcomed by a young woman called Julie who said that Cleve had asked her to look after us. She led us through a large reception room to a door which opened into the church. It was already crowded, with a lively buzz of conversation going on, and a great deal of laughter. The vibrant atmosphere struck me right away. Whoever these people were, they seemed to be enjoying themselves.

We took seats near the front, and in a few minutes Cleve appeared, accompanied by some ten young people. Cleve chaired the meeting. Some of the speakers were even younger than I am! About six students spoke – men and women – for two or three minutes each. What moved and thrilled me was the look on their faces and the freedom with which they spoke to such a large gathering. I would find that the most difficult thing in the world to do. They must have found something important to be so free from self-consciousness.

Several businessmen spoke too. One of them had had a serious problem with alcohol. He said he had completely licked the habit, much to the relief of his wife and family.

None of these people was indulging in the 'confession of sin' which Bill made such a play of that night at Betty's. They just spoke about the difference the Oxford Group had made to their small, aimless lives. Julie introduced me to some of them afterwards. They were so warm and charming – I'd like to see more of them.

November–December 1936 – Germantown

Life has certainly speeded up since my return from New York. The phone keeps ringing and I have now been introduced to the quite large Group in the Philadelphia area. Suddenly I have many, many friends.

I am trying out what the Group calls 'guidance,' taking time in silence to give God a chance to speak to me. Not that all the thoughts necessarily come from God. But surely if there is a Divine Being – as I now believe there is – He would want to communicate with His creatures?

Before I get up for breakfast every day I sit quietly and write down my thoughts. It is testing, because of my tendency to push down what I'm afraid to face. But I have set my will to be honest, and it is turning into quite an adventure. Having lived among Quakers, sitting in silence comes naturally.

One of the things that has been niggling at me is my drinking. It's not just the hangovers and the shaky hands that worry me. I feel it's self-defeating to be so dependent on alcohol for courage, excitement and meaning.

* * * * *

Early this morning a thought came to me as I was praying:

'You need to cut away all your false supports.'

This frightens me. Do I have the courage to cut loose? I would be so vulnerable – and life would be so boring. A couple of drinks do set one up.

*　*　*　*　*

I have decided to cut out all the hard stuff and stick to beer and wine.

I have also decided to return to Business School and take a refresher course in shorthand and typing. I can see this makes sense to my parents.

I understand now that the Oxford Group spreads through people. As one person finds a new life, they pass on the experience to others. I would like to be able to help people like this, to be used by God. But have I anything to pass on?

*　*　*　*　*

Last night, at a party, I met a young woman who asked me for help. She wanted to know about my experiences with the Oxford Group.

I was standing with her in a corner of the room, a cigarette in one hand and a glass of beer in the other. I began to tell her about my search for meaning and purpose, my need for discipline. But the words died on my lips. I felt a fraud. I had *not* found discipline. I was still unwilling to let God take the place of my dependence on alcohol.

When I got home, for the first time I really asked God what He wanted me to do. I wrote down these thoughts as they came:

'Not alcohol as your prop, slowly destroying you, a controlling master; but God, your Master; forsaking all, I take Him. It has kept you padded against life.'

I knelt by my bed and took a vow that I would never drink again.

137

January 1st, 1937 – Germantown

New Year's Eve again last night – and I went as usual to join the old gang. We have celebrated together for the last five years.

I found myself standing with some of the men and I suddenly told them all about my new way of life. I didn't feel at all afraid of them.

'Oh no!' they said, incredulous and amused. They treated the announcement as a joke, but they were affectionate enough and jollied me along.

'I'll give you five years at the most,' Bill said, tossing back his drink. He thought he was being wildly generous.

I didn't argue with them or try to convince them of my sincerity. I know in my heart that I have been rescued from a habit which has kept me from full development. And even these old friends are changing. We have all been through different phases, different love affairs. The association is not the carefree one it used to be. Some are bored. There are jealousies. Partners have been exchanged. We have all used each other, and are beginning to discard each other.

November 1937 – Germantown

Almost a year has gone by, quietly. I've been busy with Business School and meetings of the Group in Philadelphia.

I have now dismantled the small bar I used to have in the corner of my studio bedroom. The cocktail glasses and shaker, the gin and whiskey bottles have all gone. I'm keeping to my vow. I've also thrown out all my cigarettes, since they seem tied up with my will to do what I want to do – regardless.

I don't see so much of Betty now, or the Andersons. Since New Year's Eve we have drifted apart. I feel a little uncomfortable about this, but now I have many new friends in the Group.

Quite often I find myself wondering about Dreiser. Did he ever manage to finish *The Stoic?* I think one of the reasons my secretarial work tapered off was because he became bogged down on this book. I haven't seen any news about him for a long time, and there used to be so much.

Looking back, I feel more and more uncomfortable about the arrangement we had at Mt. Kisco – Helen, Dreiser and I under the same roof. What shakes me now is how unaware I was of what it really meant. I was so absorbed in my own relationship with Dreiser, and so self-centered, that Helen's situation never really impinged on me.

I haven't seen anything of Peter Perrot either – I hear he has moved to New York. Richard has finally got a divorce and remarried. Since my talk with Mother, I feel ashamed of those years, particularly because of her suffering. I am treating these men friends as a closed chapter.

However, the thought of Peter can still excite me. Of all the men I have known, he is the most intriguing, because the most mysterious. I still don't know what he really thought of me, but why did he send me those poems? It was clear that his wife and family were paramount to him. Was he sincere about anything?

I keep wondering what the Group means by 'absolute purity.' It seems quite far upstream to me. Yet more and more I am beginning to feel uncomfortable about my free and easy sex life.

*　　*　　*　　*　　*

I have made two wonderful new friends – a very charming couple – Charles and Margery Haines. They are part of the Philadelphia group, although obliged to be away a good deal. Charles is another of those mentioned in *For Sinners Only*. He comes from a Quaker family and it was his mother, I now realise, who was Nana's best friend. Wyck House, one of Germantown's most historic homes, has belonged to his family since the eighteenth century. Margery has a warm, outgoing personality and a gift of seeing the more amusing aspects of life. It is nice to be with people who have such flair for living.

They led an Oxford Group meeting in our house

forty people came, and both Mother and I spoke, telling about our new relationship. To my own surprise I wasn't really nervous. I knew what I wanted to say, and speaking alongside Mother gave me great satisfaction.

*   *   *   *   *

The other weekend, Mother, Warner and I went to a Group 'houseparty' in a hotel at a seaside resort in New Jersey. Warner has been looking at me strangely all year, trying to figure out why my lifestyle is so different. He has been working as an air-conditioning salesman, after a stint with the Quakers in West Virginia, building new homes for miners.

During the weekend, newsreels were shown about the work of the Oxford Group in Europe as well as in America. This year there has been a big campaign in Holland, with 100,000 people attending meetings in Utrecht over Whitsun weekend. Featured in the films was a song called *Bridge-builders* – 'on sure foundations build we God's new nations.' As the 500 of us rose to sing the song together I was stirred to my depths. I felt launched on a new crusade, shoulder to shoulder with thousands around the world.

At the houseparty, Warner decided that he wanted to work with the Oxford Group too. Through his work in the West Virginian coalfields he has developed a deep interest in labor conditions and a desire to alleviate the hardships of the mining communities. Now he says he wants to do more work with the labor unions – and to help people with their personal problems, as well. There is so much bitter feeling on all sides in industry, he says.

So now there are three of us involved. Dad too seems relieved that I have mended my ways – although he thinks that Group meetings are 'rather too personal' and keeps his distance. Arthur, who has been to one or two meetings, has announced that he feels his place is with the Quakers.

*   *   *   *   *

Once again, I'm on the verge of a new adventure. After I finished my six months at Business School, Cleve wrote asking me to go and help with the secretarial work at the Group headquarters in New York. So I'll be off in the New Year!

January–December 1938 – New York

I stood on the platform at North Philadelphia station yesterday morning, watching the long train glide into the station. It finally came to a stop with a great clatter and banging of doors being opened by the white-coated porters.

I settled into my seat and leant back while a hundred memories swept over me – trips to Boston and college, all the to-ing and fro-ing to Dreiser in New York.

Julie was waiting for me at 61 Gramercy Park. I followed her through the Gothic-style hall to the elevator. On the third floor we stepped out into a pleasant corridor with bedrooms opening off it. She led me to the one I was to occupy and said she would collect me at dinner-time.

I like the room. It has simple maple furniture, twin beds, two chests of drawers and, between the two windows, a writing table. The walls are painted a soft green.

I began to unpack my belongs, aware, as always in this city, of the unmistakable background hum of the traffic, now so familiar.

I dropped into an armchair and closed my eyes, letting my thoughts wander. Six years ago I made that fateful journey to New York to meet Dreiser, and now here I was again . . . Where was Dreiser now, and Peter? . . . So strange to be in New York and not to see them. Strange too, to be embarked on this new – almost drastic – path. Where would it lead? How long would I be here? Yet at the same time I was at peace. Things felt so right . . .

My thoughts were abruptly broken into by the arrival of my room-mate. She seemed to burst into the room, carrying two suitcases, which she threw onto the bed. She is blond, short and bouncy, and was wearing a bright green

141

coat. She made the room spring to life and my heart went out to her at once.

Her name is Barbara van Dyke, from Orange, New Jersey. She immediately took charge, and I was only too glad to let her do so. She began unpacking her cases with tremendous energy, folding everything neatly into her drawers, and keeping up a steady stream of chatter and comment.

I sat on the bed, listening to her and marveling. She certainly doesn't look like a religious worker, any more than I do. Her ambition, she told me, used to be to have more boys' cars parked outside her front door than anyone else in the neighborhood!

Right on time, Julie appeared and led us down to the dining-room. She had reserved a small table for us in a quiet corner. The room was full of people. I looked round shyly and caught sight of Cleve. He gave me a friendly wave.

Over the meal, Julie told me what all these people are doing. There is a campaign on at the moment to get out a new pictorial called *Rising Tide*, with a format similar to *Life* magazine. It describes the Oxford Group's campaigns in Scandinavia, South Africa, Britain and Canada in recent years and is about to be launched in major cities around America. Many of the people here at the moment have come to New York to plan its distribution and will go out soon to promote it.

There's a permanent staff in this building too. For one thing, Julie says, there's a mailing list of 2,000 in the New York area who get newsletters every week. And there's a national mailing list of several thousand . . .

This morning Julie took me to a meeting in one of the large rooms on the second floor. This takes place every morning, she explains – a time for clearing the day's plans and discussing future moves. Garrett Stearly, the man leading the meeting – another familiar name from *For Sinners Only* – asked me to stand up and introduce myself.

*　*　*　*　*

My first job is dealing with book orders, down in the basement. People are writing in from all over the country for the books that I've been finding so helpful myself. I do lots of filing, typing of replies, even packing up books.

A young man of about my own age has taught me the ropes – simple enough. He's the youngest son of Bishop Logan Roots, former Bishop of Hangkow, China. He's easy to get along with, with a nice sense of humor. I like the job, and it's not too taxing, but quite interesting. And I'm beginning to feel secure, as if I belong here.

Cleve drops in every now and then to see how I'm doing. He's kind and encouraging – my heart beats a little faster when he appears. Oh dear!

But I work hard enough to fall into bed every night and sleep very soundly – and our day starts early.

The alarm goes off at six a.m. I feel annoyed, but Barbara reaches over cheerfully and turns on the light between our beds. I sit up in bed and reach for my Bible, and gradually a sense of peace and order begins to steal over my soul. It helps to start the day in this way, with plenty of time to meditate and pray, and to talk over with Barbara the things that are on our minds. At the very least, it's a way of letting off steam, rather than bottling up our reactions.

Barbara's a good foil for me, so straightforward, blunt and practical, and breezy as well. She gives me a sense of proportion.

*   *   *   *   *

I have been moved to an upstairs office. Today Cleve came in and asked me to put stamps on a large pile of envelopes. I set to work enthusiastically and soon finished the job, congratulating myself on my speed.

Cleve returned and looked at the completed pile. 'This will never do,' he said, 'you've not taken the trouble to put the stamps on straight.'

I felt a sharp pang of hurt pride.

'Never mind this time,' Cleve went on. 'They'll have to go out. But next time, remember.'

I sure will!

* * * * *

Of course, I'm falling in love with Cleve. It was bound to happen. He's the first 'good' man I've come into daily contact with. But I wouldn't dare flirt with him. It's amazing – the men are with us all the time, and yet they don't flirt.

I hope I'll find fulfillment in this life – even love and marriage? Above all, now, I want a real marriage, with a husband I can look up to, and God at the center. If only I could have that, I'd go through almost anything.

Sometimes when I go out for a little fresh air and pass a cafe or restaurant and smell the fumes from the bar, the warm, pungent smell beckons. I see the dim lights, the snug interior and hear the chatter of voices and the clink of glasses . . . It tugs at me, but I hurry by, stopping my ears and eyes. I've not drunk alcohol since I made that vow in Germantown and I know I'm a goner if I don't stick with it.

* * * * *

The other morning when I was just about to cross the street in Greenwich Village, I saw a tall, heavy figure coming towards me. He was wearing a hat pinched together at the top . . . It was an unmistakable silhouette. I ran towards him, calling his name.

His face lit up as he saw me coming. We stopped in the middle of the street, where fortunately there was no traffic at that moment, and exclaimed at the encounter. More than seven million people in New York and I meet Theodore Dreiser.

'Can you come and have a cup of coffee?' he asked.

'Of course.'

We found a small cafe and sat at a wooden table. We

ordered coffee and Danish pastries and then stared at each other.

'Tell me all about yourself,' he said. 'I have thought of you so often.'

I poured it all out; the trip to Europe; my mother meeting the Oxford Group while I was away; reading the books and my decision to accept this way of life.

He listened quietly. I could see he was moved and interested. He did not belittle in any way the validity of my experience. I think he knew something of what it had cost me to set out on this road.

'I used to worry about your drinking,' he said. 'You went too far. I didn't know how to help you. This may be the way for you.'

He questioned me about the philosophy of the Group, especially about the four standards. But when I tried to explain absolute purity to him he laughed, yet not mockingly. He seemed to admire the idea of uncompromising standards and to recognize that they helped people to discover the truth about themselves.

'But it's not for me,' he said. 'I could never accept such a thing.' He told me that he has taken an apartment in Greenwich Village for a while. *The Stoic* is still unfinished and he continues to plan for *The Bulwark*. Once again I could see how he admired 'goodness' in a rather wistful way. Yet he feels that goodness is helpless in the face of the evil in the world.

I tried to explain that this is exactly the point of the Oxford Group – not to be 'good,' but to be effective in fighting evil because one's own motivation is right.

But I fumbled with my explanations. I didn't know how to explain it all to him, apart from what has happened to me personally.

We parted, saying nothing about a future meeting.

* * * * *

Today the following letter arrived from Dreiser:

145

Hotel Park Plaza
50 W 77th Street
NYC
Jan 15

Click Dear,

I was so pleased to hear from you. I've thought of you plenty – just as though nothing had ever changed and so I'll continue to think. I'm interested by and sympathetic towards what you tell me of the Oxford Movement. I've read of it of course, and know some people, you among them – who are gripped by it.

Alas, honey, I'm one of the irreconcilables as you know.

I was brought up in the Catholic faith but it meant nothing to me. My sister Sylvia is a Christian Science healer with patients, but somehow – well, I could argue about it for years. What I did love in you was your enthusiasm for the Universe with all it contained – good and evil – and your poetic rhapsodies annent *that* still run in my mind. You were, and I suppose always will remain, something like a fresh wind, blowing here and there, in the alleys as well as the gardens of life, and remaining sweet of heart. You used to accuse me of roaring violently against this and that but with no enduring rage or evil intent, and I often think you're a piece of cloth off the same bolt. I insist there's no real badness in you, anyhow, I hope not. I used to denounce you to your teeth – but not elsewhere, as you know, and yet I never really believed that I was justified in so doing.

Rather you were colorful and erratic, and gay and wistful, and courageous enough as life goes – and I wish so much you could remain so. If I were anything but *lunacy personified* I could keep you content with life I know – partially so, anyhow. But being what I am, Ah – the devil.

Dear, I hope you're a little happy. How much I wish that. And you'll never be anything but what you're entitled to be by reason of youthfulness of heart, sweetness of mind and the right we all have to dream – if we can. Write

146

me again, I think of you so often in that Quaker dress you put on once. *Lovely* was the word for *Click* in that.

Give my regards to all please.

T.D.

I've been sick. Flu: a little. Now I'm up again.

I'd like him to meet some of my new friends. It will have to be someone with a broad outlook, who knows about books.

* * * * *

In the end, I decided on Garth Lean, a young journalist, not long out of Oxford, who works with the Group. He's not a conformist and he has an easy manner, a sense of humor, and a certain shrewdness.

We met Dreiser for lunch at a restaurant in Greenwich Village. The conversation was easy, and exploratory. I'm sure Dreiser was expecting a religious type, but he met a man of the world. They discussed a variety of world issues.

Dreiser is very anti-British, because he sees Britain as an imperial power. But Garth Lean doesn't fit into any stereotype. And I could see Dreiser warming to him. I said very little – happy to see them getting on so well and to be with Dreiser again.

* * * * *

Yesterday I ran into him again, just as unexpectedly. He stepped out of the elevator at the Gramercy Park Hotel just as I was about to get in.

'I liked your friend "Lean Garth," ' he said, teasing me, and headed off for some appointment.

I'm glad he is so open and sympathetic. But I have doubts about his willingness to 'change.' He's always been so reluctant to submit to any discipline, even the Communist Party, and I can't think he'd find the discipline of God any more palatable.

* * * * *

I've made a very helpful friend, Cleve's sister, Mrs. Margaret Hicks Williams. She and her husband live on the other side of Gramercy Park and I go to see her whenever I can. I've discussed my feelings about Cleve with her. I've finally accepted that although he's a supporter and friend of mine, there's no romantic element in it.

Since I was a child I've always lived with the image of some loved one in my heart, who gave excitement and meaning to my life. In the short intervals when I haven't been in love, life has felt stale and boring. It's as if I have to pour out my feelings on some central figure.

Now, after learning the truth about Cleve, there's no one. But I'm beginning to see – dimly – that this central position in my heart is meant to be occupied by God. As I have begun to obey God's laws, my faith has grown stronger. I needed something to shake me out of the extreme self-centeredness I had nurtured for so long – and the Oxford Group put things clearly enough to do so.

January 1st, 1939 – New York

Last night was my first New Year's Eve away from my gang. I saw 1938 out with a large group of my new friends, at a special service in Calvary Church.

Many memories began to sweep over me as the hour before midnight closed in. I was on my knees, taking Holy Communion, when the bells pealed out. I could hear in the distance the horns and whistles of the revelers. At one moment I felt a touch of sadness – yet not really sadness, only a gentle melancholy – as I knelt there, shut away from the drunken mobs in the crowded streets. No, I didn't really want to be with them. The search for merriment now needed an effort and so had lost its point and spontaneity.

It was a beautiful and haunting hour, taken by Mr. Shoemaker. At one point he suggested we sit in silence and see what thoughts we might get for the coming year. That marvelous sense of unity and peace, which comes when a large crowd of people are quiet together, settled down over

148

the congregation. The air seemed to throb with a mystical presence.

I prayed for next year – and gradually my thoughts focused on a single point: that I should sell my radio-victrola machine, my most precious possession, and give the money to the Group. After all, it was a gift from Richard, who was a married man.

At the end of the silence, Mr. Shoemaker suggested that any of us who would like to might write on a piece of paper, unsigned, any decisions we had taken. I wrote mine out and put it in the plate which was passed round.

It was a costly decision – but at the same time, I felt peaceful about it.

January 1939 – New York

We have news that Frank Buchman – who started the Oxford Group – is coming to America in the spring, bringing with him about a hundred people from all over Europe. A series of big meetings are being planned.

I do so wonder what he will be like? I'm looking forward to meeting him – but will I be shy? I have heard and read so much about him. He grew up in Allentown, Pennsylvania, a small, rural community. It is interesting to realize that we drove through Allentown every summer on our way to Eagles Mere. I was always impressed with the flowers planted around the street lights in the quiet old squares.

Dr. Buchman's conviction comes from his own experience. Although he was a minister of the Gospel, he hated six men who had refused him adequate financial aid for his hospice for poor boys in the slums of Philadelphia. On a visit to England some years later, he heard a woman preaching in a chapel on what the Cross of Christ meant to her. The way she put it was so vivid and clear that he felt deeply convicted about his hate and wrote to each of these men asking their forgiveness. The experience freed him and taught him the concept of beginning with oneself rather than pointing a finger at the other person. This simple Christian truth became an integral part of his message.

The other day I had to type a speech he made recently in Sweden. Some of the phrases he used had an astringent, challenging quality about them which shook me up.

'I know what some of you would like out of the Oxford Group,' he had said, 'a nice comfortable awakening . . . but if we stopped there, I should be sorry . . . Revival is only one level of thought. The next step is revolution. It is uncomfortable. A lot of Christians don't like the word . . . The thing you have got to decide is between you and God. Write it down if you want to. It is a deed, like the transfer of property – so you turn over your life to God, for full and complete direction . . .'

The Oxford Group is now known as 'Moral Re-Armament.' The 'Oxford Group' was always a bit of a nickname and in a world where moral and spiritual re-armament is so badly needed, the new name expresses better what we are about. It seems particularly apt at a time when Europe, faced by the rising power of Hitler and Mussolini, is becoming nervous about her ability to defend herself.

* * * * *

There's an air of excitement in the building now. The phones never seem to stop ringing, the elevators fly up and down, people come and go. The place is full of laughter and joy.

March 1939 – New York

As I came down in the elevator yesterday I heard a deafening roar. The automatic doors opened and I stood there gazing out at a remarkable scene. The lobby was packed and deadlocked by two crowds of people welcoming and arriving, each pushing towards the other. In the middle of it all I saw one man, quite tall, thick-set, balding, wearing glasses, with a rosy face, and a large sharp nose. It was Frank Buchman. He looked exactly like his pictures.

Everyone was trying to shake hands with him, and he was greeting each one by name, grasping some by the shoulders and shaking them, seizing the outstretched hands. I pushed my way out of the elevator and stood there, merged into a solid wall of humanity, which was slowly easing itself through a double doorway into the reception hall beyond. Finally everyone got through. Half a dozen armchairs were arranged on a low platform along one side of the room. Dr. Buchman took a seat and called out to several friends to join him.

He sat relaxed looking out at us where we waited, row upon row, in happy expectation. A hush fell over us.

I found it a very moving moment. Dr. Buchman has something very hard to define. I, like everyone else in the room, was eagerly waiting to hear what he would say. He spoke to us very openly. I was prepared for a more religious discourse, but he talked about the situation in the world as he sees it, the dangers of Communism, of Fascism, and of materialism – 'the mother of all isms.'

April 1939 – New York

The whole tempo of life has speeded up here since Frank's arrival. I sometimes find myself working the mimeograph at midnight! But I enjoy it – it's so exciting!

We are planning a series of meetings – in New York, Washington and Los Angeles. The first will be here in New York, next month, at Madison Square Garden, which seats 12,000. Each day we meet to discuss who will speak, what songs will be sung, who should be invited.

I can feel my horizons stretching as I listen to the new arrivals speaking about their countries, some of them under threat from Hitler's armies.

Frank Buchman looks just as I expected, but in other ways he is different. He isn't a charismatic leader, not a 'leader' at all, in one sense. He's always trying to get other people to talk and to take the initiative. Often he just sits at the back of our meetings, listening.

He's changed my childhood concept of religion for ever. My faith then was so vague, emotional and unrelated to my life, it never impinged on my conduct. One thing that he says, which has impressed me, is that accepting what is wrong in society and oneself, rather than fighting to cure it, makes us who call ourselves Christian ineffective and unconvincing.

I find myself wanting to attract his attention and win his approval.

* * * * *

After all my father has told me, I find it interesting to be working with so many English people. Quite a few of them are involved in the publicity side of the meetings, writing press releases and taking photographs. Others are from labor unions, and some are from the peerage!

Yesterday I took dictation from one of them, a young journalist with fair curly hair and mischievous blue eyes, and an Oxford accent. When he had finished dictating he made a teasing remark about America having been a British colony.

'You didn't need to burn the White House,' I flared up.

He looked astonished.

'Did we?'

'Oh yes, during the war of 1812.'

It was clear he'd never even heard of the war of 1812!

* * * * *

Another of the British arrivals is a small, white-haired lady with bright blue eyes, who carries a large black handbag and wears sturdy, lace-up walking shoes. Her name is Annie Jaeger. I've noticed her because she's always at the center of a lively group of people, young and old, men and women.

I've discovered that she's a widow, who used to keep a small shop in Stockport, England. She and her husband didn't have an easy life together. Because he had a German name, he was persecuted during the 1914–18 war, and Annie's mother was against the marriage. They quarreled a

Cleve Hicks. 'A round face
and merry blue eyes,
bubbling with joie de vivre.'

The mass demonstration for the moral re-armament of America, in Madison
Square Gardens, New York, May 1939

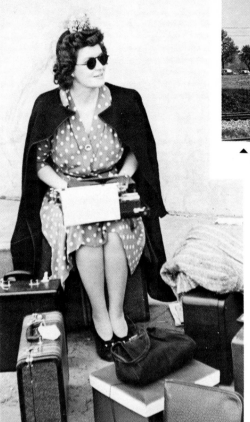

On the road with my typewriter, 1941

▲ 'We drove in a cavalcade of cars with trucks of equipment bringing up the re[...]

▲ Bill Schaffer, shipya[...] worker, 'black-hai[...] and black-browed, wit[...] suspicious scowl on [...] face. His wife is t[...] barely five feet high [...] flashing brown eyes [...] she is known [...] "Dynamite".'

Bill Jaeger (center) with colleagues. 'Short and stocky . . . I don't know if I like him or not.'

Frank Buchman. 'There's an alertness about Frank, and about those who work closely with him. I think it comes from their inner discipline.'

'When we opened the door the room was ringing with her laughter.' Bill's mother, Annie, receives visitors in her wheel-chair at the Henry Ford Memorial Hospital, Detroit, during her last illness. Bill stands behind her to the left.

With Bill after our marriage

With Fred

lot – especially over their lack of money. By the time he died, Annie had become a bitter woman.

Then something happened to Annie's only son Bill, who was studying in London. He came home one Christmas holidays and told her that he'd met the Oxford Group and made a new start in applying Christian standards to his life. He told her in detail where he had gone wrong in the past. His direct, specific honesty shocked her at first, but as they talked together on a new level, she faced up to the needs in her own life, especially her bitterness and fears over money. She was a regular church-goer, yet she had to admit her heart was heavy. Finally she admitted to Bill that she felt she, too, needed to change. At three o'clock in the morning she knelt down with Bill and gave her life anew to God. She says she looked so different after this decision that within a week twelve neighbors had come in to see what had happened and to ask her help with their problems!

When her son left college he went to work with the Oxford Group in the East End of London, a vast area of working-class homes and poverty. Annie sold off all her belongings and went to help him. They wanted to help workers find an idea big enough to answer exploitation everywhere. Annie says this begins in the home. Together they got to know hundreds of people, including leaders of the unemployed.

I'd like to get to know Annie better, since she seems so popular. I wonder why she is? At the same time, she makes me feel a bit uncomfortable. I think she may think me a bit soft – which is certainly what I feel when I compare myself to people like her.

*   *   *   *   *

For some reason these days I have found my thoughts turning towards Peter Perrot. Betty has given me his business address. He isn't too far away.

For several days I've been wrestling with myself. I could so easily lift up the receiver and telephone his advertising company. My heart races in excitement as I day-dream about

153

our reunion. What would he make of my present lifestyle? And yet I know it might be fatal for me to see him – like opening the door of an airplane when it is in flight.

*   *   *   *   *

In the end I decided to write to him. Just as I was starting, Annie Jaeger came along and sat down beside me.

'Writing a letter?' she asked.

'Yes,' I said, wishing she'd go away.

'To whom?'

'A friend of mine.'

'Is it a man?'

'Yes.'

'Is he married?'

'Yes,' I said slowly, looking back into her eyes.

'Well,' she said firmly, 'we have a name for women like that in East London . . .' And she got up and walked away.

I sat there dumbfounded, my cheeks blazing. How did she know? No one had put it so bluntly before. Marion had tried, but Annie had called it by the right name.

Her words cut in deep. They hit my pride as well as my conscience and seemed to release thoughts which I had always pushed down before. It was a cruel and heartless thing to take another woman's husband. Peter couldn't belong to me. It was really underhand stealing to try and get things started with him again.

Slowly I tore up the letter and threw the pieces away.

*   *   *   *   *

I have sent word to Mother that she can burn all my letters from Dreiser. There must be hundreds in the big box in my clothes closet . . . I gulp a little at the thought, but I am doing this for Mother's sake. All that side of my life is gone forever.

154

July–August 1939 – California

A busy four months, with a lot of traveling. The Madison Square Garden meeting, on May 14, was a tremendously stirring event. I sat with my father, half-way up the hall, which was filled with raised tiers of seats facing the large platform where the speakers and representatives of different countries were sitting, many of them in national costume.

Then on to Washington, in June, for a meeting in the Constitution Hall. President Roosevelt sent a message, which was read by the Senator from Missouri, Harry S. Truman: 'The underlying strength of the world must consist in the moral fiber of her citizens. A programme of moral re-armament for the world cannot fail, therefore, to lessen the danger of armed conflict. Such moral re-armament, to be most highly effective, must receive support on a worldwide basis.'

Then we all headed across the country to California, where a mass meeting is to be held in the Hollywood Bowl, a natural amphitheater in the Hollywood hills seating 30,000.

A society lady arranged a special train for our journey. The trip took three days and three nights. As we approached the desert, the railway cars were stifling. The British especially suffered from the heat. Since all the windows were open, the black soot poured through the fine mesh screens from the three locomotives pulling the train.

It was exciting arriving in Los Angeles and learning that we were to stay in a hotel in Hollywood. I kept wondering what movie stars we might see.

But our hotel has turned out to be far from romantic. I have a room facing onto the street and every few minutes a trolley car goes rattling by our window. The only interesting feature is the palm trees lining the street. Not a movie star to be seen – although I hear that Jeanette MacDonald is going to appear on the speakers' platform on our big night.

*　　*　　*　　*　　*

Secretaries were needed to man a makeshift office under the stage of the Hollywood Bowl and type up the speeches for the press as they were made. I volunteered. It seemed the thing to do, although it meant missing the glamorous, exciting spectacle we had watched being rehearsed for the past few weeks.

And so, last night, we were driven out to the Bowl just as the sun set behind the Hollywood Hills. I stood on the sidelines with my typewriter taking in the amazing scene. Already the place was a seething mass of people.

As darkness fell, four huge spotlights were turned on, stabbing into the sky, symbolizing the four standards. On the great stage, covered with its shell-like canopy, the speakers, guests, musicians, people in national costumes were gathering. I saw Frank there and Annie Jaeger, who was to be one of the speakers. I couldn't help wondering if she was nervous. She looked so small among all those VIPs.

The whole thing was like a scene from the Arabian Nights and it was quite a wrench to tear myself away and go down into our office with its harsh electric light and rows of wooden tables...

The evening was a triumph and even hidden away and typing non-stop I felt a great exhilaration in being part of it.

*   *   *   *   *

Living in the middle of such a large crowd of people, of every conceivable type, I am often tempted to compare myself to others; to wonder how I am doing and hope I am regarded favorably. I have a real craving to prove that I can do well in this work – be loyal, work hard, be willing to learn – but my emotional nature often gets the better of me. One person who seems aware of my struggles is Annie Jaeger. She is becoming a good friend of mine. Ever since her strong words about Peter I have felt she wants to help me. There is a real care in her.

The other day, I left a meeting in tears, because I felt left out of a special occasion that was being planned. We were meeting in somebody's home and I ran upstairs into an empty bedroom. A moment later Annie came in with one of my friends and put her arm around me. That made me cry all the harder.

Then suddenly Annie said, 'Could it be a bit of jealousy?'

I stopped crying abruptly, jerking up my head.

Then I nodded, knowing she had hit on the truth. As I admitted it a sense of peace stole over me.

'Let's pray,' said Annie and we all three knelt down beside the bed and did so.

I went back with them into the meeting with what felt like a miracle in my heart.

* * * * *

We have been holding a World Assembly for Moral Re-Armament with about a thousand delegates, from many countries. It opened in Monterey, California, and the final sessions are taking place in San Francisco as part of the World's Fair.

Yesterday I ran into Dreiser again in the swirling World's Fair crowds. How strange! This is getting to be a joke! Is it fated?

I waved to him, but he gave me a negative signal and disappeared among the milling throngs. I stood wondering what to do – he had looked worried. I went on into the meeting I was heading for, but after an hour I came out. Dreiser was waiting for me.

'I couldn't speak to you,' he said. 'I had to stay with my friends, but they've gone on now.'

We sat on a nearby bench and chatted. He asked after Warner. I told him about the Assembly. He seemed curious and sympathetic.

'We could look in at the meeting,' I said.

He said he'd like to, so we went in and listened for a while. Warner joined us, and came out with us again when Dreiser wanted to leave. Dreiser made no comment about the speaking, but greeted Warner with affectionate warmth. Then I gave him my latest address and we said goodbye.

September–October 1939 – Seattle

Our cavalcade had reached Seattle when the news broke.
Hitler has marched into Poland – and England has declared
war on Germany!

Even for me, an American safely at home in my own
country, the news has brought a throat-tightening thrill of
fear and dread. But for the French, Norwegians, Danes,
Finns, Dutch and British working with us, it is traumatic.

I was typing in a small office at our hotel base today.
Frank has just arrived from Los Angeles and all day long I
noticed the Europeans coming and going from his suite.
Their faces were grim. Some, I saw, were in tears.

Today most of the overseas workers left for their home
countries. It was an emotional farewell as they lined up to
say goodbye to Frank and climbed into the waiting bus. I
stood on the sidelines, deeply moved. What will happen to
them? Will I ever see them again?

*　*　*　*　*

The declaration of war has brought a strange muted waiting
period. Seattle is six thousand miles from London, more
from Berlin, and it all seems far away. I find I am still colored
by my father's – and George Washington's – views about
not getting involved in European quarrels. Their wars have
been interminable.

Nevertheless I do feel deeply about what the war must
mean to all my British friends. Annie Jaeger is still in America
and I continue to see a good deal of her. Her son is engaged
in morale-building work in the East End of London.

*　*　*　*　*

I've had a note from Dreiser, referring to our meeting in San
Francisco. 'I always wonder about you,' he writes. 'Why
don't the Oxford crowd get up a real, dramatic movie – a
modern *Pilgrim's Progress?*'

March 1940 – Seattle

I have to admit that I'm beginning to feel a little lost. There is now only a small group of us left in the city. Most people have gone down to San Francisco to join Frank. Annie has gone with them. There's not much need for secretarial work.

Two of those staying on are Bishop Roots – father of the man who initiated me into the book work in New York – and his daughter Frances. They have taken a small apartment and I've been living with them. We have become close friends. Frances is a gifted pianist and I sit by the hour listening to her playing. We discuss books and the art of writing and I have told her about my life with Dreiser. With all this leisure to think, I am beginning to get an urge to write again.

April–May 1940 – Germantown

Frances and the Bishop have agreed that it might be a good idea to pay a visit home and to start on my book. At least it'll get it out of my system. I feel now that I should make Peter Perrot the central character.

*   *   *   *   *

It is so wonderful to be back in our dear old house with all the books and open fires and comfortable way of life. I certainly am no longer bored living quietly with my parents. Far from it. They have become the most precious people in my life.

*   *   *   *   *

Each day brings terrible news of Hitler's blitzkrieg across Europe. The stories and photographs in the papers of the flights of the refugees, the bombings of the Luftwaffe, the sickening, heart-breaking plight of thousands of helpless people take a central position in my thoughts. I even put

159

part of the current situation into the end of my novel, having Peter returning to France to join the army.

July 1940 – Germantown

Frank has gathered his troops at Lake Tahoe in Nevada to assess the situation. I keep getting letters asking me to join them. The letters give some idea of what is happening at Tahoe. People are finding a deeper change in their lives, facing up to places where they could have done better. Warner is there and he writes enthusiastically about it all. They are doing their own cleaning and cooking, living in cottages or tents.

I feel shy and apprehensive at the thought. I am sure I would find such a time uncomfortable – too challenging. I have not compromised my new way of living since I came home, but just now I prefer to live quietly.

October 1940 – Germantown

I have finished my novel and typed it up. I am going to send it to one of the MRA workers who I think will understand it. His name is Sciff Wishard; he is married, with two children. I don't really know him, but I have noticed him because he has, to a marked degree, that air of happiness spiced with a debonair humor which is such a hallmark of the Oxford Group.

I am still getting letters from Tahoe, which describe the spiritual deepening that has developed among the 120 of them there in the quiet rustic beauty of the forest and lake. Out of this 'rebirth,' as they put it, a patriotic musical revue has been written, *You Can Defend America*. It has already been performed around the state of Nevada.

October–December 1940 – Washington D.C.

I have come to Washington to discuss my novel with Sciff. I'm staying in the house that the Wishards share with another family, the Blakes. Between them they have five small children.

After breakfast today we discussed the novel. Sciff praised my writing style, but he finally came out with, 'You don't know much about men, do you?' I was speechless. I looked at him and found his eyes regarding me with a twinkle of amusement.

'Why don't you stay on with us for a while?' he suggested. 'There is lots to do here and you could do some typing for me.'

*   *   *   *   *

I've been here a month now, and I'm enjoying the lively family life. Helen Wishard has been very understanding. The three of us sit and talk in the evenings. They were at Tahoe and tell me many stories of what took place there. They often speak of Annie and of her son Bill, who is now in America.

*   *   *   *   *

Today was a red letter day. A large group connected with the revue has arrived in Washington. I went along shyly to a meeting today and met up again with some of my old friends.

Six of those I'd always looked up to as 'leaders of MRA' opened the meeting. They each spoke humbly about what they had learned at Tahoe, especially about their need for a deeper touch with God, admitting simple feelings of ambition, jealousy, competitiveness.

I was shocked and shaken. Suddenly these people were on my level. They were just like me. My heart rushed out to them.

The larger group stood up and began singing some of

the songs from the revue, harmonizing beautifully. The words and music were thrilling and deeply moving. Tears streamed down my cheeks. All I want to do now is to stay here and be part of this marvelous family.

* * * * *

My last day in Washington. I have seen a performance of the revue. It lived up to my expectations with its catchy music and talented cast. Its theme is 'sound homes, teamwork in industry, a united nation.' It is fast-moving, with often humorous sketches interwoven with song and dance. As always, I was carried away by the music.

I'm going home with my faith deepened and with a desire to play my part in a more responsible way.

I have also accepted that the novel doesn't quite make the grade.

December 1940 – Germantown

I came back home to attend Arthur's wedding, which took place just before Christmas. The one I call my little brother is the first of us to be married. The wedding was a real Quaker one, the bride in blue. Her name is Mary. She is very beautiful, with long blond hair, also warm and outgoing. The event brought some of my self-doubts and anxieties back to the surface. Barbara came over from New York to give me support and gave me up-to-date news of everything, the most important being the rehearsals of the revue going on there, to prepare for an extensive tour of New England in the summer.

May–June 1941 – Germantown

Frank Buchman has come to Germantown with a party of forty. Mother has invited three of the visitors to stay with

162

us. Frank is staying with Charles and Margery Haines at Wyck House.

Today Mother invited Frank to tea, with as many of the others as he liked. About twenty came. We had tea in the garden under the hemlock trees. Dad came home from the office specially. I made brownies – but to my shame they turned out to be very tough, though no one seemed to mind.

After tea I drove Frank back to Wyck. Before we left I picked a rose and gave it to him. We drove off with him holding it in his hand.

*   *   *   *   *

Our three house-guests talk a lot about the show, and today they asked why didn't I join it. The thought excites me, and with some trepidation I agreed.

As I drove along one of the streets this afternoon, a car drew up by me at the traffic lights. I saw Frank's smiling face at the window. 'I hear you have decided to be an actress,' he called out. Then he was gone.

June 1941 – New York

I have come over to New York and gone into intense rehearsals and at the same time have been catching up with my old friends, all of whom are in the show. They've been telling me about some of the deep times they all went through in Tahoe. Two of the people they mentioned were Annie and Bill Jaeger – who, they said, helped many people.

Madeline Spafford, one of my secretarial friends, has been doing some typing for Bill and says he works you very hard, but at the same time takes a real interest in you. Another friend who's worked for him says much the same. I've made a mental note about the hard work – it would seem wise to avoid working for this man at all costs.

June–July 1941 – Hartford, Connecticut

You can Defend America has hit the road! Yesterday about forty of us set off on our New England tour. We drove in a cavalcade of cars with two trucks of equipment bringing up the rear. The lead car set the speed and we all had to stay in line – no room for individualism!

We have been invited to different places by state governors and by the Civil Defense Councils which are springing up all over the country. We are now called a 'morale-building group.' The show emphasizes the need for America to understand the Nazi threat and arm against it.

Our first stop is Bridgeport, Connecticut, where we have been invited by the Bridgeport Brass Company.

*   *   *   *   *

Yesterday we were hard at work rehearsing when there was a loud commotion at the back of the hall. Suddenly everyone dashed off the stage to meet four newcomers, one of whom turned out to be Bill Jaeger.

I've been really curious to meet him, though I'm not quite sure why. Not to be outdone, I joined the circle and looked with interest at this person so many people have described to me. He is short and stocky and was wearing an old raincoat, a bent hat crushed down on his head, and carrying an armful of newspapers. He has observant blue eyes, a rather large, straight nose, a firm, jutting chin and a manner which has a warm greeting for everyone.

I don't know if I like him or not. He isn't exactly an Adonis and there's all that talk about hard work. But there's a certain authority and commitment about him, like his mother.

There was no more rehearsal after this and we all went along to the church where we were to have our evening meal. Long trestle tables had been set up under the trees. After I had collected my food from the buffet I looked around for a place to sit, and seeing a space next to Bill Jaeger, squeezed myself in there.

To my surprise after a few minutes he got up and left. Why?

*   *   *   *   *

It hasn't taken long for Warner to meet up with Bill Jaeger and I notice that they are often together, deep in conversation. There's quite an interesting group around Bill – several former shipyard workers from Scotland and, from the management side, Charles Haines, whose family business, Lukens Steel, gives him good connections with the steelworkers' union.

These men seem to have a lot to talk about and, judging from the shouts of laughter which punctuate their 'huddles,' as they call them, they seem to enjoy themselves immensely. They are beginning to be known as 'the labor team.'

*   *   *   *   *

The other day, after rehearsal, I saw Bill walking along the street, for once alone. I caught up with him, using a sisterly interest in Warner's welfare as my excuse. Bill assured me that Warner is fine and that he's going to introduce Bill and his friends to the men he knows at Bethlehem Steel plant.

I feel I've registered with Bill as Warner's sister, which for some reason seems very important, although I'm not really interested in the work Warner's doing. I do feel sorry for the people who do the dirty work to keep the rest of us in comfort. But I still don't understand why Eleanor and Dreiser used to get so angry with me about this.

August 22nd, 1941 – Bar Harbor, Maine

My 32nd birthday today! I'd kept quiet about it, just telling one or two close friends. We only arrived in this beautiful summer resort last night. We're going to put the show on here, too.

This morning as I walked along the dirt road bound for

165

a planning meeting, Frank caught up with me with some friends. He took my hand lightly in both of his and, along with the others, sang 'Happy Birthday to you' to me, very quietly.

I felt warmed and touched by the gesture – on such a busy day.

November 1941 – Germantown

We have finished our New England tour. After Christmas we are to start on a tour of the Southern States.

Meanwhile the whole crowd has arrived in Philadelphia because our show is to be put on in the Academy of Music! I could hardly believe my ears when I first heard this – to me the Academy is practically a temple of the arts. The thought of our revue playing there shocked me a little at first, although it has had many good write-ups in the papers.

Jack Kelly is on the committee of invitation. All my life I have heard my father speak of how Kelly rose from humble beginnings as a bricklayer to become one of Philadelphia's most wealthy and influential citizens. His main claim to fame is as a champion oarsman – a winner in the 1920 Olympic Games.

December 5th, 1941 – Philadelphia

My heart was in my mouth as, dressed for the opening scene, I stood behind the curtain listening to the buzz of conversation as the Academy filled up.

Word was brought back to us that every seat was taken.

Then the curtain rose and we were on. I hardly dared look at the great auditorium – with its circled tiers and boxes, its red velvet seats, its gold and cream paint, its huge crystal chandelier – holding three thousand of my fellow Philadelphians.

At the end of the show a tremendous burst of applause broke out. So it had gone all right.

166

December 6th, 1941 – Germantown

We were having a quiet Sunday at home after last night's triumph. About 4 p.m. I went down to the kitchen to make some tea and turned on the radio. Suddenly the program was broken into and the announcer gave the news that the Japanese have bombed the U.S. fleet stationed at a place called Pearl Harbor. Evidently it was a devastating attack with heavy casualties.

I flew around looking for my father and found him taking a nap in his room. I shook him awake and gave him the news.

Suddenly the whole atmosphere of our lives has changed. Roosevelt has gone on the air. We are at war with Japan. More than ever the theme of the revue turns out to be relevant.

February 1942 – South Carolina

Frank often travels with us these days and we meet with him the morning after each performance to discuss how it went. I find these occasions inspiring. It's like being part of a large, closely knit family, with all our individual foibles and personality traits. Frank is like a father – though rather more firm than my own father.

Through these meetings he tries to 'train' us, to open our eyes to what we are really like and to the realities of the world. I find what Frank says a bit shocking sometimes. He can be so astringent, so different from the soft, kindly approach of the Quakers. He certainly isn't sentimental. He is a realist, especially about human nature, which as he often points out, is tough. Because of this realism, he has a way of getting to the root of people's needs, the blind spots most of us are unaware of.

There's an alertness about Frank, and about those who work closely with him. I think it comes from their inner discipline – their energies are channeled into thinking for other people and about the great issues in the world, rather than into worrying about themselves. I wish I could get to be like that. I keep feeling I have so much to learn, which is probably a good thing.

March 1942 – Orlando, Florida

I find the sun here almost hypnotic and I've been longing to get a chance to soak it up. So yesterday a friend and I decided to skip a meeting and go to the beach for a swim.

We were walking along happily with our bathing suits when a car drew up beside us. I recognized the smiling faces of some of the labor team. It was one of the Scots, Duncan Corcoran, who spoke:

'Where are you going?'

'Swimming,' I said.

'Swimming?' said Duncan. 'This is a revolution. Get in!' He grinned and so did his companions. My friend and I looked at each other rather guiltily and meekly complied.

They somehow made room for us in the car and we drove off towards the meeting hall. I was squeezed into the front seat and Duncan engaged me in conversation.

'What do you do?' he asked, turning to gaze at me in all innocence.

'I'm in the show,' I said hotly.

'I know that,' he said. 'We all are. The show's a small part of it. What else do you do?'

'I work on costumes.'

'Costumes!' he snorted. He gazed at me in mock ferocity. 'But you also type, don't you?'

'Yes,' I said.

'We sure need a good typist, don't we boys?' he said, addressing the carload. Their response left me in no doubt.

We eventually arrived at the hall. After the meeting I was heading off for an early lunch, when Bill Jaeger, Duncan, Warner and about three others of their crowd all surrounded me. Bill was the spokesman this time. He said Duncan had told him about our conversation, and how would I like to go along with them now? They were about to call on the Brewery Workers' union to invite them to the show.

I looked at their eager, rugged faces; all of them – except Warner – men who had known hard times and real poverty. The faces were shrewd and friendly and alight with humor. I felt as if I were being kidnaped, but the situation held out a certain interest.

'All right,' I said.

And before I could change my mind I was bundled into one of the two cars, heading for 'The Labor Temple,' the local headquarters of the American Federation of Labor.

Since I knew nothing about labor unions and have never been interested in them, I was a little apprehensive about what role I might be asked to play.

There was no problem. We stormed up the wooden stairs and burst into a large packed room. Everyone turned in their seats to stare at us as we came in. My brother seemed to know the chairman of the meeting and was given a few minutes to speak. He described the aims of the show, told how we had been invited to Florida, gave the names of labor leaders who had already endorsed the show and told them where they could get tickets. Bill and Duncan also spoke briefly and the rest of us were introduced.

The applause as we left was very friendly.

We visited four more unions to issue invitations, then got back into the cars and headed for a restaurant and cups of tea. My new friends produced long typed lists of the different unions and the names and often the home addresses of their officers. No one paid much attention to me so I ate my sandwich and listened to their plans.

I seem to have been adopted. I've already taken dictation from both Bill and Duncan.

*   *   *   *   *

Neither Annie nor Bill drive, so chauffeuring is another job that needs to be done. Annie has already enlisted four other young women, besides me, to take her on her calls and in the process to learn the ropes of the labor work. Annie calls it 'going on the knocker,' which is what she used to do all over East London, getting to know hundreds of women there.

I hear more and more about her convictions on home life. She feels everything starts in the home – for bad or good. Men who exploit their wives and wives who nag and browbeat their husbands create an atmosphere of bitterness which spills over into the working world. On the other hand, when husband and wife sort out their lives together and with their children, Annie believes, it is a big step towards building a just society.

One of those learning the ropes from Annie is Rosamund Lombard, a real New Englander, who has been working with the Jaegers since the show was in Boston last year. Another is Polly Anne Eastman, whose father is the President of the Chamber of Commerce in Los Angeles. Then there is June Lee, a miner's daughter, whose marriage broke up not long ago after ten years. The Jaegers took her on when they were in San Francisco. The fourth is Edith Shillington, a young British woman.

*   *   *   *   *

Yesterday Annie asked me if I would drive her around to call on three women she had met after the show. 'We'll take some flowers,' she said as we walked towards the car.

This was my first visit ever to a worker's home, and I couldn't help wondering what I would say. We finally arrived at a neat little brick house in a long row of workers' homes. This woman's husband is a union secretary.

Annie rang the bell; in a moment the door opened a crack, and a woman's face peered suspiciously at us. Her expression changed quickly as she recognized Annie and received the bunch of flowers Annie held out to her. We went inside and found a small, neat living-room.

Annie told the woman about her life back in England, how she had been a church-goer, but how this had not helped when she and her husband had had bitter quarrels over money. She described what a difference it had made when

170

she was honest with her son about her fears and bitterness. The woman was completely won over. In no time she was describing her own life, the problems her husband was up against, and how she often felt neglected because her husband was always out.

I sat quietly listening, feeling it wisest to say nothing, though Annie drew me out a little.

All through the visit, Annie poured out such warmth and care that I could see that the woman would never be the same again. She had become a friend for life. I learned a great deal, just being there. What so many people want is real care and genuine friendship – and yet so often they are not given it.

Annie has whole address books full of the names of women she has met. You can see her working on her letters every spare moment she has.

March 1941 – Atlanta, Georgia

We often go to speak to unions too and to invite their members to the show. The other day it was the Hatters' Union. Unfortunately, I didn't think of wearing a hat. When we arrived at the organizer's office, she took one look at me and exclaimed, 'It's people like you who are putting our girls out of a job!' She flew to a cupboard, and, to my horror, descended on me with a huge, pea-green cartwheel hat, which she proceeded to force down on my head. I had no intention of wearing anything so unbecoming, so I quickly took it off again. Just as quickly, the union official forced it back on. This could have gone for some time, but Annie came up to me and said, in no uncertain tones, 'Stop thinking about yourself.' So I submitted. I spent the next hour walking through the factory trying to be gracious, while the pea-green model kept slipping.

April 1942 – Florida

Every day our labor task force meets, to go over the names of the union presidents and officials we will be calling on in the cities we visit. Through listening carefully I am gradually beginning to understand more about the unions – and about Bill.

The other day he told us about the first American labor convention he attended – the United Mineworkers' held in Cleveland, Ohio, in the spring of 1940, shortly after his arrival in the U.S. It was a period when many of America's labor leaders – including John L. Lewis, the miners' President – believed America should keep out of the war. The Communists encouraged this line, because of the Nazi-Soviet Pact. All around the convention hall were placards saying, 'The Yanks are not coming' and 'The war is a war of British imperialism.'

I've learned that in spite of the war, Bill was allowed to come to America in 1940 by the British Government because they were worried about American labor's confusion over the war.

Bill feels strongly about the need to remake the world and the ordinary man's part in that task. He will discuss this with anyone. He feels it is essential to have better economic and technical conditions, but that when you have them, it is only half the coin; the other half is people's motives, and if they don't change, other changes won't work. You need both.

Part of my new secretarial duties is to make copies of the many public endorsements of the show made by labor leaders after they have seen it. For instance, James A. Duncan, Grand Lodge Representative of the International Association of Machinists in Seattle, sent this message to 1,500 of his friends in labor circles:

'As we struggle to overcome injustice in a world about ruined by dishonesty, selfishness, greed and hate, we must surely see that to change these conditions we must first change men. This can be done. MRA points the way.'

The United Steelworkers sent a delegation to the

performance in Philadelphia and came away so keen on it that they want us to put it on at their first international convention in Ohio in May.

May 1942 – Cleveland, Ohio

The performance for the steelworkers turned out to be a stirring affair, ending with a standing ovation from the two thousand steelworkers and their guests. Their president, Philip Murray, came up on the stage at the end of the show and said, '*You can Defend America* is a call to action against the divisive materialism which is our unseen enemy. It must appeal to all whose fight is for a new social order as an essential defense of American democracy.'

This is very encouraging as we prepare to move on to Detroit, a very tough city, run by the motor barons, including Henry Ford Senior, and the powerful automobile workers' union. The huge car factories are now manufacturing the weapons of war – tanks, especially. Detroit has become known as the 'arsenal of democracy.' I am driving up with Warner, Duncan and Bill.

May–June 1942 – Detroit

The drive turned out to be another education for me. Bill and Duncan kept up a non-stop conversation about the political situation in the unions in Detroit. Apparently there is constant warfare in these unions between the Communist and socialist factions.

Because of the war, high productivity is essential. At the same time, there are many unofficial strikes. Bill, Duncan and Warner want to get to know the leadership in the unions, on the factory floor and in management, and work to build trust between them. They have found that where workers and management apply the principles of MRA, production often increases. Often even a changed home life improves the quality of work done and the atmosphere in the factory.

* * * * *

The show opened to another packed and enthusiastic house. Mr. and Mrs. Henry Ford were in the audience.

Ever since arriving in Detroit, Annie Jaeger has been extremely busy speaking at various luncheons and receptions. She has met Clara Ford several times.

The other day Annie complained of feeling unwell, and looked it. One of the leading doctors at the Henry Ford hospital arranged for her to have tests. We are now shaken to learn that she has cancer. Mrs Ford has arranged for her to have a room in the hospital, so that she can have the best of care during her operation.

* * * * *

We have a list of three hundred labor men and women in the city and are planning which ones to see.

For the first week, another secretary and I stayed at a boarding house, catching the bus every day to the MRA office. I find downtown Detroit depressing – so many cheap eating houses and bars, so many pasty-faced men and women. There seems to be little architectural plan to the city as a whole. I gather the city grew up around the car factories as they were built.

Then two days ago I got a message to move out of the boarding house by four o'clock next day and bring my things to the office. I had been offered bed and breakfast by the wife of a businessman who had just seen our show.

By now I have accumulated several suitcases of belongings, plus a typewriter and a hat box. How was I to get all this stuff from the boarding house through busy city streets to our office several miles away? Automatically I thought of Warner, who has a car. I telephoned the office and left a message that he was to get in touch with me as soon as possible.

Hours went by. I kept telephoning but no one had see him, or knew where he was. I began to fume. Where was my brother when I most needed him?

Around 4.30, having made one last phone call, I gave in and ordered a taxi. (Taxis cost money and I don't have much.) I had to lug my heavy suitcases into the cab, and on arrival, carry them one by one up the long stone stairway to the office.

Just as I got the last piece through the door, flushed and perspiring (it was a very hot day), Warner walked into the room.

I rushed up to him.

'Where have you been? I've been trying to find you all day.'

'I've been driving Bill Jaeger around,' he replied innocently.

I boiled. Driving Bill Jaeger when his sister needed him so badly! I was about to let fly, in spite of the fascinated spectators, when Bill walked in the door.

I forgot Warner and turned on Bill.

'I hate you, I hate you, I hate you!' I cried, by this time quite indifferent to what anyone might be thinking of me. 'And I hope Rommel wins!'

Bill, to my annoyance, took it all calmly. His blue eyes looked steadily back into mine, direct, kindly eyes.

I turned away. What is it about this man and his mother? I always feel challenged by him.

Warner stepped in and took my arm and said he would drive me to my new home. The matter was dropped and never mentioned again.

*　*　*　*　*

We have a massive follow-up job to do with all the people who saw the show.

Yesterday, June and I drove out to Dearborn to see if we could meet Rita, the wife of one of the shop stewards in the Ford Rouge plant, a nurse and union member whom we had met after the show. She had impressed us as a real fighter.

In the short time we have been in Detroit, we have already heard many blood-curdling stories of the early struggle to unionise the mighty Ford empire, when 'goons' were used to beat up the pickets, and a line a mile long stretched outside the plant. Rita had told us that she was on that picket line and had had to nurse many a bloody head. There are now 30,000 union members in this one plant alone.

We knocked at the screen door of the little house and Rita answered – a thin, wiry woman in slacks, holding a cigarette.

With some of the workers we visit I now find it quite easy to strike up a friendship. But with others, like Rita, I feel self-conscious, aware of the difference between the privileges I used to take for granted and the battle they have had to fight. But June, with her mining background, understood what Rita had been through.

It wasn't only Henry Ford and the management that Rita was bitter about. Her eyes flashed when she described her husband – always drunk, she said.

June told about her divorce and how she had put all the blame on her husband for walking out on her. 'But I accept now that half of it was my fault,' she said. 'I wasn't easy to live with. I even went to see him and his new wife and gave them a tea-set I knew my husband had wanted to take with him when he left home. We all ended up in tears and friends. It moved a deep bitterness out of my heart.'

'And you,' Rita asked, looking at me with curiosity. So far I had kept quiet.

I told her about the way I'd lived, how Mother had apologized to me and what honesty had done for our family.

'I'll make a pot of tea,' said Rita abruptly. Shortly her three children came in from school, a boy of thirteen and two younger girls, and then her husband, a great, tall, lanky man, who seemed very surprised to find us drinking tea with his wife.

*   *   *   *   *

Bill goes to see his mother every day, and different ones of us take turns driving him to the hospital. The first day I went I was a bit uneasy. I didn't want to see her suffering and was planning to speak in a hushed, sick-room voice.

But when we opened the door, the room was ringing with her laughter as she talked to a group of nurses and other visitors. Then Bill plunged into the room, hurrying across to the window, where she was sitting in an armchair. They teased each other and laughed. My solemnity was out of place, as were my fears and dread of her illness.

The Jaegers have a special kind of courage. I think it comes from their unselfishness and their love for each other, which isn't self-indulgent.

July 1942 – Mackinac Island, Michigan

We have been given the use of an old, unused hotel on Mackinac Island, for a token rent of one dollar a year, as a place where we can gather during the hot summer months and bring people for training in MRA. The building was in a terrible state of dirt and neglect, but a group of us descended on it and cleaned it up. Behind the hotel is an old barn, which we are using as a small theater.

September–December 1942 – Detroit

Now that summer is over, the revue is moving on to the West Coast for the winter to play to the workers in the Lockheed and Boeing aircraft factories in Los Angeles and Seattle. Annie is still very ill in the hospital, and Bill is staying on in Detroit to be near her. Today we had a meeting to decide who else should stay on for the winter to continue the work here. I felt a strange feeling of relief when my name was mentioned. Why? Interesting.

Seven of us are to stay – Rosamund, June, Bill, Warner, Tom Gillespie, who writes articles for the labor papers, George Vondermuhl, who once worked for the International Labor Organisation (ILO) in Geneva, and myself.

*   *   *   *   *

We have settled down to a busy routine. We meet every morning to plan the calls for the day, write articles and letters, listen to Bill's diagnosis of events around the world in the last twenty-four hours, and to discuss them together.

This is one of the highlights of the day for me. Reading the newspapers – definitely more than one in order to be able to sift the truth – Bill considers a basic essential. We must live into the world, he says, understanding the forces at work and the personalities and motives of the leaders who have such influence over our destinies. If we become knowledgeable along these lines, the people we meet will realise we are not talking pie in the sky.

The papers Bill reads each day range from the conservative Hearst Press, the *New York Times* and the Detroit papers, to the various union papers, the *Daily Worker* and the Communist press. I find comparing the different papers a revelation. Dreiser was involved with certain left-wing periodicals, but I was not really interested in politics in those days. Bill relates left, right and center to an ideological battle for people's minds. I feel excited and stimulated listening to him. His approach is lifting my understanding of MRA from a purely personal lifeline for my own needs to a concept which is relevant to the world scene.

And I am discovering that I love being around Bill. In his orbit, life becomes an adventure. He has such a zest for the battle. For him, morality is not a set of rules, but living in a clean, caring and disciplined way in order to be used by God to bring about a just society. And can there be justice unless the ordinary person changes?

In visits to Annie and in our times together, we keep learning more about Bill's background and what it was like to grow up in a northern England mill town with very little money. It isn't easy for us to envisage that small shop in Stockport and the life there. The Jaeger family often had to live on twenty-five cents a day for food. Bill has told us how insecure it always made him when there were fights between his parents over money. And many a time I have heard Annie telling the labor families who come to see her how much she regrets that her husband died before she was cured of her bitterness. 'I so wish I could have said "sorry" to him,' she tells them.

The Jaegers knew persecution, too. During World War I, anyone with a German name was suspect. The police even came to the house to ask questions. Bill's father had been born in Liverpool, but his grandfather had come from Germany. Bill was beaten up by other boys on his way home from school. Annie told us how he came home from school one day and said, 'Mother, am I a dirty little German?'

But it wasn't all grim struggle. We hear also how dozens of people kept popping into the small house for cups of tea and for musical evenings when Bill played the parlor organ and everyone sang. When Bill was sixteen, he trained and conducted his school orchestra. To this day, he knows the whole of Beethoven's First Symphony by heart and can play it straight through on the piano.

Every evening now, after a long day's work and before setting out on our evening calls, the seven of us descend on one of the many cheap, but excellent eating establishments in Detroit. What Bill loves beyond all other items on the menu is fish and chips. And there is always an urgent request to the waitress for a bottle of vinegar, which he pours over the whole plate.

※　　※　　※　　※　　※

The other night, Bill had a phone call to say that Frank had had a stroke and could be close to death. We were all really shaken. We did not go out next day, but sat together in our basement office, praying for Frank and talking quietly together. It seemed inconceivable that we could lose Frank at this point – he is only sixty-four.

That evening Bill telephoned Saratoga, where Frank was taken ill, and was told that Frank was holding his own. Today we heard that Frank has passed the crisis and is beginning to show some improvement, although his right arm is paralyzed.

February 1943 – Detroit

I have been in bed with a heavy cold for a few days. Yesterday afternoon I was quietly reading when I heard voices and footsteps outside my room. Then came a knock. The door opened to reveal Warner, Bill and Rosamund, all smiling broadly. Bill asked me if I was getting well and encouraged me to hurry up and come back to work. The three of them seemed in high spirits. They gave me some news of what they were doing and then waved goodbye.

The door closed and I sank back on my pillows and gazed at the ceiling, feeling strangely excited and exhilarated. I even felt my cheeks were flushed. Then I burst out laughing.

Of course, seeing my brother wouldn't produce this effect, and certainly not seeing Rosamund. So that left Bill . . . !

How strange. I lay there a long time, smiling to myself and thinking about him, seeing in my mind his broad, stocky figure, his lined face, the battered hat and raincoat, the newspapers that are always under his arm, his direct blue eyes that seem so wise and so kind.

He is a most unusual man. There is no doubt about that. It is hard to put a label on him.

I began to feel very peaceful and happy – and also amused at myself.

After a while I got up and drew the curtains and turned on the lamp. It was quite dark outside, and turning into a wintry night. I opened up my book and began to read.

*   *   *   *   *

A week has gone by. I am well again and back at work.

I am very conscious of Bill in a new way. Several times I've offered to do his letters for him, but he's only thanked me and explained that June can manage. I don't like that bit of information too much.

My imagination has already carried me ahead into the unknown future. Suppose I married Bill. What would life with him be like? Would we be very poor? Would I have to live in a small, cold, uncomfortable, damp worker's home, eating dripping and tripe, without all the things I take for granted?

*   *   *   *   *

Warner has gone into the army, so now we are just six. Tommy and George have both been classified unfit, and Bill has been given special clearance to continue his work in the war plants.

March 1943 – Detroit

The days come and go – so full, so busy. I go through my work, typing, filing, driving cars, visiting people, the daily meetings. But as soon as I wake up in the morning, I find myself thinking of Bill. Something is happening – something I can't stop. All the familiar sensations of falling in love, which I have been through so many times in my life – is this different?

I would never want to hinder Bill or hold him back; I admire him and what he is doing so much. I know how selfish I can be. And so sometimes, in my mind, I have tried to give him up. But I can't. He has invaded my life.

It's true Bill and I are from different backgrounds, but it doesn't really bother me. Indeed, I think his poverty has fashioned a character which is not only steadfast and dependable, but generous and full of humor as well.

May 1943 – Detroit

Yesterday we celebrated Annie's sixty-fifth birthday in her hospital room. She's been there for almost a year now. The birthday was quite unusual – so many nurses, orderlies, cleaners, doctors came to wish her a happy day and to have a piece of the cake we had baked for her.

A terrible disease is at work in her. I come to see her

almost every day and marvel at her spirit. She is near death, but thinks only of others, and of the God who she believes is leading her even now – especially now.

Yet I know that alone in that hospital room at night, she must be tempted to doubt and to be afraid.

July 1943 – Detroit

We see Rita's family regularly. She is a real ally now. Her son, now fifteen, is spending his second summer at Mackinac where he has joined up with others of his age group to produce a play about teenage life.

Only Jack, his father, remains elusive, and Rita gets impatient and critical. However, when we run into him, he seems to be genuinely fond of us and grateful for the change in Rita. So we have decided on a rather drastic plan. We will shanghai him and take him to Mackinac. This should be comparatively simple as long as he has had enough to drink, which is often the case. We commute between Detroit and Mackinac every weekend, escorting union groups.

*   *   *   *   *

Last Friday night, George and Tommy went to the cafe where they knew Jack would be. They found him already the worse for wear after his nightly binge, but were able to persuade him to come outside and get into their car. They helped him into the back seat, where he immediately went to sleep, as they headed for Mackinac, three hundred miles away. Jack only awoke next morning as they came to the end of their journey.

By that time, he was cold sober and astonished to see where he was. Rita welcomed him, gave him breakfast, then took him to the barn where their son was acting in his play. As the curtains parted and Jack saw his son on stage, he was riveted. Finally we saw him wiping his eyes. At the conclusion he stood up, went on to the stage, put his arm around his son and spoke from his heart. He said that at last he understood what he needed to do and how much his family meant to him.

September 1943 – Detroit

I have met a couple of real firebrands from Philadelphia, Bill and Irene Schaffer. They came to Mackinac for an industrial conference over Labor Day, last weekend. I was there with a group from Detroit.

Bill Schaffer is President of the Shipyard and Marine Workers' Union in Cramp's shipyard, an old family firm whose vice-president is a friend of my father's. So it seemed natural for me to look after them when they arrived.

Bill Schaffer is a striking-looking man, black-haired and black-browed, with a suspicious scowl on his face.

His wife is tiny, barely five feet high, with flashing brown eyes. Schaffer told me she is known as 'Dynamite' – christened by John L. Lewis, the mineworkers' president, when she fought on the picket lines in the early days of the union.

They were so colorful, so natural, so open in their reactions, that it was easy to be friends. By the end of the weekend, I felt like a member of the family. Irene had opened up to me and poured out all her grievances against the world – and against her husband, Bill. 'He's never home,' she said. 'How do I know what he's up to?'

Over the weekend, a play was performed, *The Forgotten Factor*, set in a factory during a clash between labor and management. I sat beside the Schaffers watching it, and I could feel their deep reactions as they saw acted out on stage the very situation they knew in their own lives: distrust and hatred of management, bitterness and suspicion between husband and wife, outside forces exploiting the divisions to get control of the union for political ends.

Before they left at the end of the weekend, Bill and Irene spoke to the conference. He told how he had grown up in the slums of Philadelphia and had had to fight every inch of the way to survive. He said he had never believed he would find employers like those he had met at Mackinac, men

183

whom he could trust because they were honest with him. On that basis, he said, he could work together with the management at Cramp's, and keep the men building the ships so needed in the war.

Irene followed him. They had been married ten years, she said, and had finally decided to get a divorce, but this weekend had made them decide to try again. It would mean so much to their two little girls.

＊　＊　＊　＊　＊

It looks as if I will be seeing more of them, for we are all moving to Germantown! The doctor has told Bill that it would now be best for Annie to leave the hospital and spend her last months in a home where she can be surrounded by loving friends. As there is a campaign planned for Philadelphia this winter, my parents and I have offered her our home. Bill is to move in as well – along with five others.

December 1943 – Germantown

June, Rosamund, Polly-Anne and I look after Annie. People come to see her every day, just as they did when she was in the hospital, and go away heartened by her. We have put extra leaves into the dining-room table to seat the twelve people who now live in the house. In a remarkable way, Mother and Dad have turned the home over to us.

At least once a week, some of us go to visit the Schaffers, about an hour's drive from home. Schaffer has introduced us to his most trusted lieutenants. One has two wives – both living in the same house! Another is a former bouncer, who has been in Sing-Sing prison. He has lost a finger in a fight, and causes us much merriment when he talks about MRA's four standards and holds up three fingers.

Schaffer also has a bodyguard, a huge ex-boxer, with a high squeaky voice – and an unusual interpretation of our work. 'Before I met MRA,' he says, 'I used to hit everybody. Now I just hit the ones Schaffer tells me to.'

All these colorful characters crowd into the Schaffer home to discuss union business and hear our news. Then about eleven o'clock, Irene brings in huge platters of sandwiches and pots of tea.

January 1944 – Germantown

Irene has told me about one of her big problems.

'The phone rings,' she said. 'I answer, and an unknown voice tells me that he has seen Bill out with a redhead the night before. Then he hangs up.'

After a call like that, Irene rages. Is it true or not? 'What I do,' she went on, 'is wait for him in the dark until he finally comes home and then I hit him over the head with a broom when he starts upstairs.' She has also made a sign and hung it in their front window; it says, 'Schaffer's Restaurant – Meals served at all hours.'

We've discussed the anonymous phone calls. She admits that Bill has enemies, especially now that he has a more co-operative attitude towards management. Those who are trying to get power by fanning division don't like his new attitude and may be trying to turn her against him.

She's begun to see that it's hard for Bill to have to fight his wife as well as the disruptive elements at work. But she doesn't know if she can trust him. 'He's hurt me so much, for so many years,' she says.

February 1944 – Germantown

It's been wonderful to have Bill living in our home and be able to see so much of him every day. I am glad that my parents have had a chance to get to know him. A little while ago, I was talking about him with Mother and she expressed it this way: 'Heart, brain and character make him a peer among men.' I was deeply moved.

It is quite clear to me now that Bill also cares for me. We are drawn to each other more and more. But I find I am still shy about telling Annie how I feel, wondering if she would approve, knowing me as she does.

She is very weak now, and we all know the end must be close. When I was passing her door a few days ago, I noticed she was alone, and I suddenly ran in and knelt beside her, putting my head down close to hers. She whispered to me and I felt quite sure then that she knew.

*   *   *   *   *

On the night of 13th February Annie lost consciousness and slipped away.

She so often used to quote from the old gospel hymns she sang in her youth. When she became too weak to talk, someone suggested we might sing to her. June and Polly Anne both have fine voices, and during the last forty-eight hours of her life, they sang those old hymns. It was wonderful to see the expression of peace steal over Annie's face as soon as she heard them. During most of those days and nights, Bill stood by her bed, holding her hand and calling out to her.

Since she died, Bill has had letters from over five hundred families who have found a united and happy home life through meeting Annie. Frank wrote: 'She lived the miracle of being poor yet making many rich, of having nothing, yet possessing all things.' And a United States Army chaplain, who came to her funeral but had never met her, wrote, 'the first truly Christian funeral I have ever attended . . . There was more simplicity, more unpretentious love, more godliness that I have seen for many months. It was like sunshine, fresh air and freedom to an imprisoned soul to enjoy that fellowship.'

September 1944 – Germantown

After Annie's death, Bill and the others left our house, and the Clark family returned to a more settled way of life. Frank came to Germantown again and celebrated his birthday at Wyck House.

The International Labor Organisation was meeting in Philadelphia at that time. Bill brought two of the British labor delegates out to our house for tea – Dame Anne Laughlin of the Tailor and Garment Workers and Florence Hancock of the Transport and General Workers. I believe it was the only American home they had been invited to.

Bill also made good friends with the Chinese workers' delegation. Two of them came to Wyck House to meet Frank. They also came to dinner with us at the home of the publisher of the *Philadelphia Labor World*, one of the papers which carries weekly articles from us.

I see the Schaffers often, and they have become two of my best friends. They love to tease me about me feelings for Bill.

We were all at Mackinac again this summer, and the Schaffers came up for a weekend. Bill and I spent most of our time with them; at one point Schaffer confessed to Bill that there was no redhead, but that he had lost a lot of money on the horses.

'I'm scared to tell Irene,' he said.

One morning when we were sitting with them, Irene suddenly said that she was sorry for her hot temper, that it must have made it hard for her Bill.

Schaffer then blurted out about the horses. Irene began to splutter, her eyes blazing. She was getting ready to strike back, but suddenly caught herself and gave her husband a big smile. 'All right,' she said. 'But no more.'

This painful honesty built a trust between them. I do rejoice to see how devoted they have become.

January 1945 – Washington D.C.

I have been asked to help edit the news-sheet we put out from Washington, so have come down here. I enjoy the work, although I sometimes wish I could be with the labor group, who are now based in Los Angeles.

Everyone knows that Bill and I are in love, but what will be the outcome? I can't be sure. He has never spoken of marriage. This may have something to do with the war. But I find the uncertainty very testing.

April 18th, 1945 – Washington

Today it has happened. The war in Europe is over. As with its beginning, it is hard to take in. Immense relief, but at what a cost. After the news, my friends and I sit quietly, then each of us prays. We know so many who have lost their lives, and we know of others locked up in concentration camps.

August 1945 – Mackinac

I'm back here for the annual summer conference and very moved to see Bill again.

Then yesterday the morning meeting was interrupted by an announcement; by the order of President Truman, atomic bombs had been dropped on two cities in Japan. This means the war in the Pacific is over.

It was suggested we sit in silence and live into this momentous news. As with everyone else in the room, I'm sure, I felt tremendous relief, but at the same time shock and foreboding at what such a bomb meant. Again the terrible cost in lives and suffering over six long years filled my thoughts.

December 1945–January 1946 – Los Angeles

I am working with the labor group again. Frank is here as well, and there is much excitement because all the men who have been in the army are about to be released.

I am staying in a small downtown hotel, sharing a room with Rosamund. As we passed by the news-stand on the way to breakfast today, I saw one of the papers with a huge black headline all across the top of the front page: 'Dreiser Dead.'

I bought one and took it to our table, pouring over it. A myriad of emotions erupted in me. He had been living in L.A. for the last few years, with Helen, whom he had eventually married after the death of his first wife.

When we met together that morning, Bill and Warner had already seen the paper. 'You had better go to the funeral,' said Bill. How typical of him! I would never have gone on my own.

The funeral is to be in Forest Lawn, that well-known final resting place of the Hollywood great. Wherever we drive in the Los Angeles area, we are confronted with huge bill boards advertising its advantages: 'Just one call,' they say.

*   *   *   *   *

This morning Bill, Warner and I drove out to the cemetry. My heart was beating fast, as it always does before any event where I cannot be sure of how to cope. Would I see Helen? Would she disapprove of my turning up?

By the time we had finally tracked down the little chapel, we were late. We went in at the rear door and saw the place was packed. Every seat seemed to be taken. An usher took us in hand and led us up the aisle to the one pew that had a few places, the second row from the front, and I realized that we were seated directly behind Helen. I felt very conspicuous. Our footsteps had echoed loudly on the tiles of the aisle, just as the service was about to begin.

I found it a depressing farewell. Like Aramis in *The Three Musketeers* it was not 'au revoir,' but 'adieu for ever.' There was not one word of Christian faith, comfort or hope. It was a pagan burial. He was finished.

Charlie Chaplin read *The Road I came* from Dreiser's collection of poems *Moods*. John Howard Lawson, the left-wing writer, made a speech. Various others whom I did not know spoke of his writing. I glanced at Helen sitting directly in front of me, her head bowed. I knew it was a starkly desolate moment for her after all the years in which he had been the center of her life. I thought of all she had suffered from him, yet at the end, he had come home to her.

Suddenly the service was finished. I felt unable to face Helen and so, followed by Warner and Bill, hurried back down the aisle and outside into the bright California sunlight.

As we drove home, we discussed the funeral. Bill sees Dreiser as a world figure, who had a great influence on American writers during the critical Depression years and pioneered the school of American realism. Dreiser is required reading for the intellectuals in the Soviet Union, which in Bill's mind is enough to underline his importance.

We discussed the fact that several well-known American Communists had dominated the service. In his last years, Dreiser identified himself with the Communist Party, but I feel that this was less out of conviction than out of disillusionment with the tragedies and inequalities of life and with man's brutal pursuit of pleasure and success regardless of the effects on his fellow human beings. If only I could have another chance to talk to Dreiser now that I have learnt so much more. But sadly, that chance is gone.

March 1946 – Los Angeles

I am more than ever in love with Bill. He looms large in my thoughts.

It's four years now, and since I can't be sure whether he intends to marry me – or if God wants us to marry – it's not easy. I felt furious about the uncertainty last night and stormed at God. When I was quiet, God seemed to speak so clearly; 'There's nothing to stop you loving Bill, whether you marry him or not.'

I went to sleep peacefully after that.

*   *   *   *   *

We all gathered this morning, a Sunday, under the eucalyptus trees in the garden of the home where Frank is staying. There were about two hundred of us – the group which has worked together during the war years, and those who have come home from the army, navy and airforce.

Frank is planning to return to Europe in five weeks. Most of us will go with him, leaving a comparatively small group to continue the work in the States.

At the end of the meeting two of my friends stood up and announced their engagement – an American girl and a British man. They will get married before we sail. I did find it hard, listening to them. Will Bill and I ever make such an announcement?

March 18th, 1946 – Los Angeles

June telephoned early this morning to ask if I would have lunch with Ros and herself. Certainly.

As we settled in at our table I unburdened myself again to these two old friends who know me so well.

'It does make me jealous,' I said, still hating to admit it.

They only smiled.

After lunch, we walked up the street to the office, where we went every day to collect mail. As I entered the small room I saw Bill, Warner and a group of the labor crowd all standing together. Did I sense something in the way they all looked at me? Everyone seemed to be doing an awful lot of smiling.

Then Bill approached me.

'I need someone to drive me down to Santa Monica this afternoon,' he said. 'We need to make a call on the machinists' president there. Could you do it?'

I quickly agreed, and followed Bill out to the street to pick up the car. To my surprise, only Bill got in – I had assumed that one of the others would be going with us. I had never driven Bill alone before.

We started off, heading down the long straight boulevard that led to the Pacific Ocean, about twenty miles away.

Bill seemed in a very happy mood and, once when I glanced at him, I noticed he had a blue flower in his buttonhole. This seemed most strange. He wasn't the type to sport such a decoration.

We came to the wide road running parallel to the ocean. 'Turn right,' Bill said.

I did so, and we drove along under the tall, waving palm trees.

'Stop here,' Bill said, as we approached a small turn-off at the side of the road where it was legal to park.

'Stop the engine,' Bill said.

Only then did I dare to let all my rushing, whirling thoughts come into focus.

'Will you marry me?' Bill asked.

I never really answered him but just fell into his arms.

This evening we celebrated with a large crowd of our friends, Frank in the middle of it all, as well as the engaged couple of the day before.

As I said goodnight to Frank, he said, 'Now you will have to become responsible.'

I know what he means. Five years ago I was determined not to get involved with a man who worked so hard. Now I'm going to marry him. What will be asked of me as his wife? It'll certainly mean an end to the easy-going lifestyle I still prefer. I have a feeling that Frank sees me very clearly.

April 1946 – Pocono Mountains

We have had barely four weeks to travel three thousand miles across the country to Philadelphia, get out five hundred invitations, plan all the wedding arrangements and, on top of that, buy clothes and get ready to sail to England after squeezing in a four-day honeymoon! I am not too surprised. This is a foretaste of what life married to Bill will probably mean, but it hasn't left me much time or strength to savor it all, having waited so long.

We decided to be married in the same church where Annie's funeral was held, just two years ago.

Bill and I share a wish to include people. We hate to leave anyone out. So we had ten ushers and eight bridesmaids!

We asked Frank if he would give the blessing at the end of the service, which was yesterday. When the moment came, and we were kneeling together at the altar, Frank came forward:

'Whom God hath joined together, let no man put asunder.'

This was a sacrament in the sight of God, and a vow I took kneeling there, my hand clasped in Bill's. God has given me Bill, and I prayed that I will be a support to him and not a hindrance.

After the reception at the Barclay Hotel, friends drove us to the train that would take us to New York for the first night of our honeymoon, on the way to the Pocono Mountains.

We had a candle-lit dinner in the hotel restaurant in New York. I had bought a very special hat, covered with pink roses. After we had ordered, Bill produced a huge pile of telegrams from a briefcase and proceeded to read through them, reading quite a few out loud, but with his attention and eyes glued to the messages. A feeling of disappointment began to steal over me. I had bought the hat for one purpose only – that he would spend the evening admiring me in it. Now he wasn't even looking at me!

I finally burst out, 'Oh forget the telegrams! Let's just talk.'

He looked surprised, even startled, but quickly got the point.

I knew then, as I have always suspected, that my most serious rival is going to be the printed word.

April–May 1946 – London

As we rode from Victoria Station in our hired red double-decker buses yesterday, I stared in shocked silence at the bombed-out buildings along London's famous ancient streets. We finally drew up in front of MRA's London head-quarters, a row of houses in Charles Street, off Berkeley Square. A crowd of our British comrades were waiting to welcome us after the seven years' separation of the war.

A great shout went up as the two groups saw each other. There were about 180 of us arriving, and twice as many British receiving us. I heard many shouting, 'Bill, Bill,' and as soon as we stepped on to the pavement we were surrounded and propeled into the house where we were to stay.

* * * * *

I am now rarely alone with Bill, except late at night when we finally get to bed. We are constantly surrounded by crowds of his old friends, hungry for news, eager to work with him again and keen to meet me. I sometimes feel a little out of it. I know no one, but they all know Bill so well.

We've been at an endless series of receptions, tea parties and visits to the homes of his old friends. We drove by the spot in East London where Bill and Annie used to stay. There was nothing left but rubble. In fact, the whole of East London is a terrible sight – whole areas of flattened houses.

London is pretty drab and grim. Food and clothing are rationed – my trousseau, with all the pretty hats, embarrasses me; it looks so new and frivolous. People here have to save up coupons if they want something new. Electricity is rationed too, so it's not easy to keep warm.

We have one egg a week, very little real coffee. However, the MRA houses here receive regular food parcels from friends in America and Canada. Mother, in her typical way, has organized a group of housewives in Philadelphia who keep a steady flow of food going across the Atlantic – sugar, coffee, butter, jam, raisins, chocolate, tinned meat, cakes. This means we can entertain the many people who call.

Soon after we arrived, I unpacked one of our main wedding presents, a large silver tea-service, and invited one and all to join us in our rather large room for tea. About thirty people arrived the first day and packed into the room, sitting on the floor and draped all over the beds and chairs. This event has become a fixture.

As Bill's wife, I am busier than ever. It seems I have taken on not just a husband, but an army of his friends. Of course, it's Bill they all want to be with. I can't blame them for that. They're very nice to me and accept me completely, but their eyes go to Bill and stay with him.

I've made up my mind to give my heart to Britain. Not to try to 'become British,' of course, but to enter into everything, without making comparisons all the time.

✳   ✳   ✳   ✳   ✳

Today I went in search of Bill around lunchtime. He'd been to a meeting, but we'd agreed to have lunch together, and it was getting late.

The meeting had broken up, but there was a group of people standing in a circle. In the middle was Bill, expounding some great truth to his fascinated listeners. I stood in the doorway, trying to catch his eye. I even called his name, but he didn't hear me. No one noticed me. A little mortified, and with more than a touch of hurt pride, I slipped back to our room.

Half an hour later Bill came rushing through the door.

'Where have you been?' he cried. 'I've been looking for you. We'll be late for lunch!'

When I told him I had come for him and he had never seen me, he was terribly upset. He took me in his arms and apologized deeply.

✳   ✳   ✳   ✳   ✳

Much though I longed for the day when Bill and I would be married, I am finding it quite an adjustment. It was such a shock at first when our wills clashed. I'd retreat into a mood, even though in the end we always made it up.

Over the weeks, I've begun to see the cruelty of these moods – of silence no matter what Bill says. It's a way of

195

keeping control and getting back at him. I am beginning to see that it makes him feel insecure and unsure of himself.

I have to admit that I am still an emotional person and therefore cannot be easy to live with. I sense that Bill often tries to please me in order to keep the peace. This situation makes me uneasy. I don't like to feel that he is afraid of my reactions.

The other day, after one of our arguments, I suddenly noticed a deep sadness in his face. It struck me so hard that I rushed to him and threw my arms around him. I have taken a decision not to indulge these moods and I pray God will help me to keep it.

May 1946 – Stockport

We've finally managed to get away to visit Bill's relatives in Stockport. We traveled up today. I was bundled up in a wool suit and a fur coat. It may be May, but it feels like winter.

We had tea on the train. The carriages smelt of disinfectant. As the train moved northward, we left behind the lush green fields of southern England, and a harsher landscape began to unfold. I stared out the window at the scenery. At long last, I was about to see Annie's country.

We drew into the station just after sunset and stepped out. The air was soft and wet, laden with the smell of coal dust. Then a small laughing woman with white hair and blue eyes rushed towards us. It could have been Annie. It was her sister – Auntie Alice. She and her husband fairly jumped at us, embracing us, talking and laughing with such vivacity. They walked around me, taking me in, teasing Bill about his American bride. I loved them immediately. What a wonderful simplicity and lack of formality.

We started off down the street, heading for their home. Finally, through a narrow back alley, past a redbrick wall, we went in at the back door of the tiny house, one of a long row.

The little room, which we entered through an even smaller scullery, had a grate where a coal fire burned brightly.

There was also one window, an upright piano, a table, two armchairs, one or two straight chairs. There was hardly room to stand up. They showed me a front parlor off the tiny hall, both icy cold. We were led up the narrow dark stairs and shown our bedroom – also very cold, dark, and with a double bed taking up most of the space.

There is no such thing as a bathroom, and Auntie, with much gay chatter, led me along the brick path to the facilities in the back yard. I can't help thinking if it is like this in May, what must January be like? But the warmth of the personalities makes up for any chill in the weather. Nothing could have been more delightful than the endless cups of tea, bread and butter, buns and scones we ate around the brightly burning coal fire.

*   *   *   *   *

This morning we walked across to High Hillgate – the area where Bill was born and grew up. We walked about a mile, past rows and rows of silent houses. There was little traffic on the streets, petrol being rationed. No one in Bill's family owns a car, nor has ever owned one. Finally, we came to the shop. Dingy and dusty, the whole building is about twelve feet wide, and is now used for storage. It still belongs to the neighbor who gave Annie £40 for it.

Bill pounded on the door and a sharp-eyed, strong-featured woman came out; she flung her arms around Bill and shouted aloud for everyone to come. She had had no warning that Bill was back in Stockport, and she hadn't seen him for eight years.

She unlocked the door of Annie's shop and I walked inside. How small and dark it was. I saw the little counter where she would have served her customers – it was gray and dusty, and the shelves behind were empty. A door led from behind the counter into a square room. One window looked out on the brewery next door. The glass was dirty and dim. This room was like the one at Auntie's with a fireplace. Bill explained that it was their one living-room, where they ate, sat and Annie cooked. It was about eight

197

feet square. Beyond was the scullery – a small room with a sloping roof – with a sink and one cold water tap.

We went upstairs – narrow, steep wooden stairs. At the top, the front room looked out on the busy cobbled street. A tiny little box of a room adjoined it – Bill's room. It was very dark, the window looking out on the brewery chimney and on rows of houses. A maze of brick walls separated the houses, each with its back gate, its W.C., its small tiled area, which they called 'the garden.' There was not a blade of grass in sight, not a tree anywhere to be seen – only bricks and cobbles and coal smoke sifting through the soft, damp air.

*   *   *   *   *

Today, Sunday, we went to Church. I have met all the relatives now. I sensed that many a curious eye was studying the American. When it came to the collection I opened my purse, searching for a suitable contribution. The half-crown looked appropriate, and as the little green velvet bag, suspended on its wooden handle, reached me, I dropped the heavy coin inside, hearing it clink quite loudly as it landed. One of my new relatives, I noticed, was leaning forward in her seat, keeping an eye on the proceedings. I hoped I had made the right decision.

July 1946 – London

Bill's main work at the moment, with others, is in the British coalfields, where production and morale have been very low. Britain has a debt of nearly £3 billion and the mines may be the key to her economic revival. So we've been using *The Forgotten Factor*, which deals with industrial relations, a lot.

Recently a crowd of us went to the Doncaster area, where there's been quite a response to MRA's ideas, to meet miners and their families. Although it was June, it was raining and really cold. Bill and I were put up in a miner's home.

We all converged on a village hall for tea. As I stood in the rain, waiting for Bill to finish his conversation with one of the miners, I heard a voice at my shoulder; 'It's a long way from Philadelphia, isn't it?'

I turned and saw Frank smiling at me. I must have looked pretty glum – but it was nice to know that someone understood the way I felt.

*   *   *   *   *

Things really seem to be happening in Doncaster since the miners saw *The Forgotten Factor*. We heard last week that production at one of the largest pits has gone up by over half. It seems that one of the managers, who'd been a bit of a dictator, saw the play and apologized to the workers for his attitude – and this seems to have changed the whole climate at the pit.

July 1946 – London

Yesterday I went to see a doctor and have had my suspicions confirmed. The baby – whom I'm already calling Frederic, for my father – is due next February. Bill is certainly excited at the news.

We are about to set out for Switzerland, where a European center for MRA is being opened in a village called Caux, near Lake Geneva. For the first time since the war, we will all be together to plan with Frank how to bring healing to the bitterness and disillionment of the millions who have gone through six years of unbelievable suffering.

January 1947 – London

It has turned out to be an unusually cold winter – quite an initiation for me in non-American ways of life. I have spent many hours sitting on the floor huddled beside a single bar of an electric fire.

February 1947 – London

A week before the baby was due, Bill came home with a hyacinth plant which looked as if it might come into bloom any day. When I woke up yesterday morning it was in full bloom. The scent filled the room and gave me much pleasure. Every Easter Day Dad always used to give me a hyacinth plant, while Mother got a lily!

Last night, everything suddenly started up. I woke Bill. He sprang out of bed and rushed to the cupboard and began pulling on his clothes with terrific speed, ending up in his best suit, with his hair brushed, ready to get going. His anxiety about being late amused and touched me very much, but it was many more hours before we finally drove off to the hospital.

It was a boy all right!

IV

*A truth told us is harder to bear
than a hundred which we tell ourselves*

François Fénelon

December 1962 – Cornwall, England

Dark, noisy, dirty Paddington Station in London – the clatter of the porters' carts, the dingy-coated women cleaners, the dull, grayish light; not here the gleaming steel and chrome, the silent, hushed interiors of the American railway terminal.

We stood there, the three Jaegers, waiting for the night train that would take us to a new home in England – Cornwall, to be exact. Bill and I are now middle-aged; Fred is a tall fifteen-year-old American, bewildered and somewhat dismayed to find himself back in England after nine formative years in the U.S.

About ten o'clock the following morning our train pulled into Penzance. Collecting quite a pile of luggage, plus a guitar, we left our carriage and walked along the platform. In the distance we saw our host to be – hatless, a scarf knotted around his neck. He greeted us warmly.

'I wonder if we'll all get in,' he commented, coming to a stop before, what seemed to us, a really minute vehicle. 'This is our "mini",' he said, 'but we can put the luggage on the roof.'

The drive took us along the sea; many of the roads seemed dangerously narrow, bordered by stone walls on the ocean side and hedgerows on the other. I stared glumly out of the window. The sea was ever present, on our right. We passed through a series of small villages. What would our new home be like? Already I felt chilly in my American suit and thin shoes.

The tiny car bounced along the twisting lanes, then, suddenly, we came out on a raised plateau, and a huge panorama of water lay spread out below us – the Atlantic Ocean, calm now, with a gentle swell.

We drove down a narrow dirt road until we were quite close to the sea. Ahead of us we saw a white house, the sole building on the horizon.

'There it is,' we were told, 'that's Dolphin Cottage.'

In a moment we had entered a sandy drive leading to the door. Our hostess appeared, and we were led inside.

We went down the narrow hall to our bedroom, small,

simply furnished, with two windows looking out on the sea. Fred's room was delightful – a built-in bunk bed, also overlooking the sea, as good as any ship. Then we returned to the most charming room, many windows, a fireplace with a coal fire burning, a grand piano, a dining alcove, walls covered with family photographs, deep armchairs upholstered in soft pink, a crystal chandelier hanging down from the ceiling – the whole thing a charming combination of city drawing-room transported to the seaside.

Fred paced around, hands in his pockets, a look of incredulity upon his face.

'Is this where we're going to live?' he asked me. From the drawing-room window there was only the sea spread out below us and away in the distance, a thin brown road mounting a dull, rust-colored hill toward the horizon. Not a tree in sight. The horizon was naked, marked only with bare, dull brown hills, left over from the tin-mining days. It did indeed look bleak and lonely. I didn't let on to Fred that I shared his doubts and apprehensions, charming as was the room in which we were now standing.

* * * * *

What were we doing in Cornwall? To explain, I will need to go back some years.

1947–62

The fifteen years after Fred's birth had brought a lot of travel, especially for Bill. Industrial relations were urgent as Europe sought to rebuild her shattered cities and economies. At the same time there was work to do in America. This meant that the three Jaegers crossed the Atlantic quite frequently.

I didn't find the first long separation from Bill easy. In 1949, he was invited with others from MRA to visit the Ruhr, Germany's industrial heartland, where different ideologies were battling to fill the vacuum left by the war. We were apart for six months.

It was also the beginning of the everlasting packing up and moving from one home to another. I became quite good at putting down temporary roots and pulling them up again, determined each time to create a home-like atmosphere for Bill and Fred and the people we were working with.

And no matter where we were, each summer meant a trip to Caux to take part in the conference there.

I saw a good deal of Frank Buchman during these years. He often invited Bill and me to meet people who had come to see him. And I would seek Frank's advice on where to base with Frederic when Bill had to travel. One year I knitted Frank a scarf for Christmas, very long, in varying shades of blue. He received it most graciously – but I never saw him wear it.

In 1953, we were asked to move to Washington D.C. in order to give moral support to our old friend John Riffe, the steelworkers' leader, who had recently been elected Executive Vice-President of the AFL-CIO (American Federation of Labour – Congress of Industrial Organizations). Fred was six at the time and began his education in an American school.

I loved being back in the U.S., and our son quickly took on American ways.

Two years after our move to Washington, Bill and I were asked to take part in an eighteen-month MRA campaign in Asia and Africa with a musical show called *The Vanishing Island*. I had a fit and burst into tears when Bill told us we were expected to go. My parents, now quite elderly, were just about to move out of their large house into an apartment and were counting on my help. How would they manage without me? Then there was Fred, now eight years old. We had friends who could look after him, but he would certainly hate to have us leave him.

I struggled with my feelings for several days, but finally decided that I had to go, if people felt I should. (It was only later that I discovered where my inner motive had gone wrong, through my desire to please people.)

There's no question that the tour helped many people in the countries we visited — maybe even affected their history, and it was a stretching experience for me, as well as an education, to see, if only briefly, so many foreign lands. A year and a half later I finally arrived back in the U.S. I dropped in on my parents, happily settled in their new home, then went off to Michigan where Fred would be brought to meet me at the airport.

Coming in to land I stared eagerly out of the plane window and saw a small figure standing alone and motionless on the tarmac. There was something so patient, so obedient and trusting about his quiet waiting, that the sight quite stabbed my heart with a twist of pain.

'Hello Frederic,' I said, walking towards him and holding out my hand. He looked up at me. Tenderly, gently I drew his little body towards me. I didn't kiss him, not wanting to overwhelm him with my feelings; but could I hide them from him?

*　　*　　*　　*　　*

In the summer of 1959, Bill and I moved into the MRA headquarters in Washington, while Fred stayed on with the Vondermuhls, whose home we had shared since 1953. Several of the military hierarchy in the city were showing an interest in our work. Unexpectedly, I found myself in the role of Washington hostess, at first reluctantly, and then, as we seemed to be making headway with these men and their wives, I swung from my customary diffidence to feeling rather pleased with myself. I began throwing my weight around and taking charge in a self-important way.

This was our life for about six months, with many of our colleagues coming and going and taking part in our various dinner parties and receptions.

Then the bomb fell.

Frank, who I had always felt had a soft spot for me — or at least that he was amused by me and interested in Bill's and my work — sent me a letter in which he made it quite clear that I was bringing a wrong influence into the situation. He suggested that I go home to my parents for a period.

I was stunned. What he said was a mortal blow to my pride. All I wanted to do was to flee – to get out of sight. I packed a suitcase and Bill took me to the station.

As I sat on the train, bound once more for Philadelphia, I thought how these journeys were interwoven in my life – always leaving, always coming home. Twice before I had arrived home in disgrace – sent back from college – sent away by Dreiser – and now this!

Three weeks later, at his request, I went to see Frank. I was braced for almost anything. He was an old man now, in a wheelchair. For half an hour I sat beside him. I had a sense he was trying to read me, to see how I was. His voice was quiet and kindly. He seemed to be searching for something.

He asked many questions about our work in Washington. I could see he was trying to help me. But I was so accustomed to aiming to say the correct thing that my mind wasn't really free. I tried to say what I thought he wanted to hear – that I was sorry for anything I had done wrong, that I was loyal and would accept anything he suggested.

Some weeks later I returned to work, joining Bill and Fred at Mackinac, where I helped in the kitchen.

I saw Frank once more before he died. Alas, my heart was closed to him. I knew there must be something he had wanted me to learn, but all I knew was that my heart was now a stone, and I blamed him for it.

*   *   *   *   *

A few months later, in August 1961, Frank died. Mother, Bill, Fred and I went to his funeral in Allentown, Pennsylvania.

As I stood at his graveside, on a hot summer's day, I felt the significance of his passing to be momentous.

Crowds surged around all over the cemetery, strangers and friends. People were taking pictures, walking on the gravestones . . . For some it was only a curiosity – a local son come home to rest. There was such a scramble among the living, to look and see. Already there was a sense of the world moving on.

We were left.

What should we do – the three Jaegers?

I would never again hear that firm voice. I might not ever know, either, why he had taken such a strong line with me.

A relief to think he would never hurt me again. I was almost glad, really, that Frank would no longer be around.

✳   ✳   ✳   ✳   ✳

Meanwhile we were worried about Fred, who was now fifteen. We had to face the fact that we had not given him much of our time throughout this busy period. When we did see him, we found it difficult to communicate, felt a distance in him. His school grades had slipped in some subjects, and he was running with a fast crowd.

Remembering my own youth, I was frightened for him. What if he didn't manage to get into college and get a job? Was he drinking too much? And, I had to admit, I felt resentful, really, that his conduct was threatening our reputation as parents.

A friend, Peter Howard, suggested that it might be a good idea if Fred could return to his English roots. I didn't like this idea at all, but almost simultaneously friends in England wrote asking if Bill could return to work there.

We happened to know a British grammar school headmaster, John Guise, and finally wrote to ask him if he could fit Fred into his school. He agreed and offered us a home with his family until we could find one of our own. True, the school was in Cornwall, and when I looked it up on the map, the place looked really remote. Nevertheless, the move seemed right. Fred took the news with veiled interest. At least it would be a change.

And so we found ourselves in the fishing village of Porthleven, looking out at the expanse of sea and eating roast lamb with mint sauce while the Guises regaled us with

stories of gales, shipwrecks and wreckers. I could see Fred
was unimpressed. He was a city boy, to my sorrow, and
Cornwall might as well have been Siberia. But although I
didn't know it, we were all three on the threshold of new
life.

December 1962 – Porthleven

My bed is directly under the window. All last night I tossed
and turned, hearing the sea. The tide must have been coming
in, and, after all the tales I had heard, it sounded to me,
lying there in the darkness, listening to the wind and the
pounding of the waves, as if we were in for one of those
mighty storms. Each time the breakers struck and broke on
the cliffs they seemed to come closer, and I fancied the small
cottage shook and trembled. In my mind's eye, I could see
great walls of water, eating away at our very foundations.

I pulled the blankets up over my head, trying to shut
out the ceaseless sound. Surely our hosts would have warned
us if disaster were imminent. But I had seen clearly enough
that there was nothing at all between us and the sea but
these black, rocky cliffs. Of course they had been there a
long time . . .

The next day was dull and colder. As I dressed in our
coolish room, I shivered. My thin stockings and American
shoes, my suit – nothing seemed right or adequate! A fishing
village; no central heating. December; the Atlantic
Ocean . . .

I smelt a lovely aroma of toast – home-made brown
bread. We ate in the window; now the sky was gray and
lowering; the view spread out before us was gorgeous; all
tones of gray and dull blues and greens. The tide was going
out. Gulls screamed and dived from the rocks. The windows
of the house rattled from gusts of wind. A bright coal fire
glowed in the hearth. The beauty smote me, but the cold
made me feel edgy.

I happened to speak of the cold, and so, after breakfast,
I was given a paraffin stove for our room. As the housekeeper

lit the wick, the smell assailed my nostrils, taking me back forty years to our camping trips with Dad. I am a good deal older now and have no urge to rough it.

*   *   *   *   *

The pipes have frozen. We can't get a drop of water for a household of six. I tried not to feel critical when John explained that the pipes in England do freeze from time to time because they are laid above ground. So why not put them underground? Well, it doesn't often get that cold and they always have been outside . . .

When Fred heard the news he looked appalled. Even more appalled when we told him he had been delegated to go up the hill with a large container to collect water from the cattle trough in the farmyard. He didn't say much, but the look in his eye made it plain that he thought everything connected with this latest adventure of ours was close to the lunatic fringe. Nonetheless, off he went, up the hill to the farm.

Then the electric power went off. We are reduced to cooking and heating water on top of the paraffin stoves. The battle to keep clean has become intense. I have made it my main job, spending hours at the sink fighting back the tide of greasy, dirty dishes and pots and pans.

Only Fred and I are shocked by all this. Bill certainly isn't, and the Guises take it in their stride. I can't stand things breaking down. Why not make them so they will work?

*   *   *   *   *

We struggled for three days without electricity and without adequate water. Then today the sun came out. It was almost like spring – warm, gentle, balmy air hovered and breathed over everything. Suddenly I heard a trickling sound above our heads. It was water slowly emerging from the pipes in the tank in the attic. Water! Heaven had returned to earth. It might have been gold, so great was our glee. We ran around the house shouting. That night we all sat around the fire, quite contented. We were comfortable and clean again.

January–April 1963 – Porthleven

We have been on the lookout for a place to live. On our walks to the harbor and its cluster of shops, Bill and I have noticed a charming, pink house, with a large picture window. Making enquiries, we found it was empty and might be for rent.

So today we visited the landlady, a tall, thin woman. Her glance and manner were shrewd, but she was very friendly.

Directly in front of us as we entered was a red-carpeted stairway. We turned right and were in a long, lovely room, low-ceilinged, with a stone fireplace at the far end. One whole wall was the picture window I had so admired on my walks. The room was painted a soft off-white, the furniture was simple, but comfortable and attractive. A large blue carpet covered the floor.

I had to exclaim at the soft beauty of the room, and its inviting charm. The original owners, the landlady told us, were an old fisherman and his wife. When they died recently, she bought it and modernized it, but left much of its original design.

We told her about our work, and about bringing Fred to England, and how we wanted to create a home for him.

'You can have it for five guineas a week,' she said, her bright eyes looking warmly at us.

'You mean the whole house?' I gasped, my heart fluttering.

'Certainly,' she said.

*　　*　　*　　*　　*

Today Bill and I took possession of our house. We found a fire already burning in the grate, and a paraffin stove in the dining-room.

I ran upstairs to make the beds and get all in readiness

for Fred when he came home from school. As I worked I could hear the waves breaking against the cliffs – even closer here than at the Guises'. The spray hissed and the water roared and crashed as it hit the rocks.

Fred arrived. Tea was ready for him, and as his eyes took in the pretty scene, a little smile of contentment flitted across his face. We had crumpets and currant buns, and iced cakes. We three sat together, the coal fire brightly burning, with the night coming on, listening to the waves. The tide must have been rising.

I thought then what a round-about way we had come to be together like this. I sighed deeply; a new, unfamiliar sense of peace was stealing over me.

I am lying listening to the roar of the waves breaking on our cliff. Now they carry a strange reassurance. This is God's world, cut off in a way from man – at least, for me it is.

*   *   *   *   *

This morning I gave Fred a hearty breakfast. When we opened the front door, the air was filled with a wet mist, almost a soft rain. Fred turned up his collar and started off down the road for the harbor and the school bus.

I closed the door and set to work on the house. The fire had gone out, of course. So down on my knees I went, to shovel out the ashes and lay a new fire with paper, kindling and a few pieces of coal.

The postman came by on his bicycle, knocked on the door, opened it, called out my name and announced that I had some letters. Next, Mr. Orchard came by with the milk.

Then Bill and I set out along the steep narrow lane on top of the cliff to get the groceries. We found the tiny shop and went inside, a bell tinkling to announce our arrival. The wind from the sea swept in with us. It was small and dark inside, but crammed with all kinds of goods. A large man in a white overall loomed up behind the little counter. He had a thick dark moustache and his name was Mr. Hendy.

Bill said I came from America. I gave my small order,

but before I left, Mr. Hendy drew my attention to his carrots – from Texas, he said. Would I like any?

Carrots all the way to Cornwall from Texas, displayed in this tiny, dark shop, on top of a cliff, with the Atlantic ocean pounding and crashing just below us – I couldn't resist them. They did justice to Texas and to the U.S.A., being all done up in a plastic bag and of uniform size!

Mr. Hendy, with a flourish, added one and sixpence to my bill.

*   *   *   *   *

Bill has work to do in London, so once we were safely installed in the cottage, he said goodbye.

I am completely occupied all day, keeping us warm, clean and fed. Warmth and cleanliness are hardest. My bedroom in the morning is frigid – as is even more the small alcove for the W.C. The small paraffin stove in the dining room takes off some of the chill, but it doesn't reach upstairs. I spend a lot of my time building up the coal fire. Fortunately there is all the hot water I can use.

Fred is gone first thing in the morning and doesn't return until tea-time. I walk down to the harbor every day to collect a newspaper and our bread. Although I felt American and a little shy at first, I've now come to know many people in the shops and along the road.

I am learning to count every penny. Like all MRA full-time workers, we receive no salary. Ever since our marriage our expenses have been covered by contributions from friends who believe in our work and want to support it – often at personal sacrifice.

One of these regular gifts dates back to 1935 and came from a businessman whom Annie and Bill had helped in his home life. It has been paid into a bank ever since and has accumulated while we were in America. But once we have paid the rent, bought our fuel and our food, there's not much to spare. Just as well we have no car or telephone.

Bill comes down from London when he can, but Fred and I are alone in the house most of the time, although I don't see much of him either, except at meals. Then he is off, down to the harbor to meet his school chums.

In spite of the growing pleasure I receive from living in our pretty little cottage and having a quiet domestic life, I still get weighed down with fears about Fred. And the memory of the letter from Frank lies heavy on my heart. At any odd moment it pops into my consciousness and gives me a stab of pain.

I have told the Guises about the letter and also about my fears for Fred. They have taken to visiting me on Saturday nights – particularly anxious ones for me, since Fred is never home until after midnight.

* * * * *

Last night, as we sat around the fire, John suddenly asked me a very blunt question:

'Do you hate Frank Buchman?'

It was so sudden that I reeled under it. I stared back at my two friends, then looked away into the fire. A whirl of reactions, covered-over memories and events paraded before me.

'Hate?' – that was a strong, shameful word. It wouldn't be 'right' to hate a man I believed so firmly was especially used by God.

There was a long silence in the room while I struggled to sort out my thoughts.

'Maybe I do,' I finally said slowly, feeling as if I wanted to cry. Then suddenly I said: 'Yes, I do! I do hate him.'

He had smashed my pride, taken away my self-esteem, my carefully built-up confidence – I, who had been so unsure of myself.

But to hate anyone, and say that you love and serve God . . .

I began to talk to these two friends as I haven't talked for years.

* * * * *

213

Through the next weeks I move in a daze: and yet weights seem to be lifting from my heart. As I am willing to take an honest look at the facts, springs of hope seem to be welling up with a renewal of life.

The talks with the Guises continue. It is as if a cork has been pulled out of a bottle or a tightly coiled spring suddenly released. The Guises take me on long drives around Cornwall. Now the lanes are lined with banks of wild flowers, the wooded dells inland carpeted with bluebells. The air is fragrant and sweet. Rebirth is all around me.

Yet I feel such a pain in my heart sometimes, alternating with the times of peace. It is as if something is trying to be born; dying and being born – or reborn – both at the same time.

I keep thinking about the word 'hate' John used. It is a word that I never thought would apply to me. Now it does. Of course, if you suffer hurt – especially hurt pride – it's almost inevitable that you hate the person who inflicts it. And a hate-filled heart must mean a godless heart. God flees such a heart.

As I walk by the sea, clean the house, sit by the fire, I begin to admit that I have lost my touch with God, and thus, with my calling. One of the main reasons for this is that over the last years I have been covering up so much of what I really feel. In other words, I have stopped being honest. Admitting my true feelings about Frank has uncorked a lot of things. I am beginning to see how much I wanted to 'do well'. I used our work in Washington to bolster my self-esteem and my reputation with my peers. This sort of ambition rather leaves out God!

I am also beginning to feel that perhaps it was something more insidious and fundamental in my nature that most disturbed Frank – my drive to please other people, whatever the cost. This need in me meant that I ended up doing things I didn't believe in. I rarely spoke up, even when I wasn't sure about what I was asked to do. Perhaps that was what Frank saw in Washington, an unreal person unclear in her motive and her purpose. Little wonder he acted as he did.

I knew that Frank's genius was to open new life to

people by helping them to pin-point the real area of defeat in their lives. But when he finally did it for me, I resented him for it.

And it wasn't just change of conduct Frank wanted for us, but – even more important – new motivation. I *have* changed in my conduct, radically, but now this other area is coming into focus.

Along with this new understanding of myself and of what Frank was getting at, one possibility lifts my heart with a surge of joy: could all this help me to build a closer relationship with Fred? And if I find something new, what a difference it might make to Bill's life. My unreality must have been a block to both of them.

I remember Frank saying that the work of MRA must never mean more to us than our touch with God. God, not MRA, should be our security. That's just where I may have gone wrong. I have been so firmly committed to the wrong thing – to a group of people – to Frank himself. I thought this commitment of my will was my one strength, and so I stuck with MRA.

But where is God? Where is love? Where is the true me?

I have to admit that I had become a dull, hypocritical woman, all the time talking about a God who wasn't real to me. Was Frank trying to rescue me from a blindness about my motives which would have proved fatal for me and for my family?

I catch my breath. Suppose, after all, what seemed so cruel was in fact an act of love?

'Except a seed fall into the ground and die, it cannot bear fruit. . . .'

*   *   *   *   *

My son and I ate our Sunday dinner today as usual, one of our more leisurely meals. I have found myself looking at Fred with new eyes recently. I wondered what he really thought of me. Dare I ask him? We usually skirt around any personal subjects, sticking to safe ones, but both of us are rather bored.

215

'What do you find most difficult and annoying about me?' I suddenly asked him. He darted a quick glance at me, his eyes probing mine to see what I was up to.

'Do you really want to know?' he asked.

'Yes,' I said, bracing myself. 'Yes, go on, tell me.'

'Well – the way you always come out with a moralizing phrase – no matter what I say you top it and have the last word, so there's no point in talking.'

I let this sink in; it was most helpful.

'You talk in a jargon,' he went on. 'I know what you are going to say before you open your mouth.'

'Anything else?'

'You worry too much, especially about me. You're full of fear. You should stop worrying.'

That's fine, I thought, but maybe I have reason to worry. On the other hand – maybe not as much as I think. Maybe I am the bottleneck.

I gave him his ice-cream. When he had finished he sat back contentedly. 'That was a good meal,' he said.

I got up to wash the dishes and he followed me to the sink and picked up a towel. He has never done that before without a request. I asked him about the dances on Saturday nights. He began to talk and never stopped for nearly an hour. He told me about his friends, mostly the sons of fishermen in the village, and their English ways.

'They call the girls "birds" here, you know.'

'Oh, that's rather nice.'

We had the longest conversation we have had since he was a small boy.

* * * * *

The talk we had seems to have freed something in Fred, and yet I am chastened to see how often I have to catch myself as I am about to deliver a 'moralizing phrase.' It has become an unconscious habit – and all the unthinking jargon that goes with it. When I forget, Fred stares at me. I laugh and apologize.

We find we can talk now, especially about the books

216

...ornwall. 'Every day
...hen I go out into the
...he that runs along
...eside the sea, I feel that
...am beginning to walk
...ore erect – to stand up
...d face the world.'

Fred Jaeger, aged
fifteen. 'We find we can
talk now . . . What I have
longed for him is
beginning to happen.'

Frederic Jaeger, 1979

Frederic and Joan at their home in Kent

With Bill and Frederic at Knebworth

very year seems to deepen my
evotion for Bill. I am convinced
at he is the only man with
hom I could have lived so
appily and with such
atisfaction.'

The street in Stockport, England, where Bill was born

ll with Fred

Bill with my brother, Warner

Bill leading a meeting of 1200 people in East London, 1956

Bill Jaeger at the piano, in a friend's house in Washington, D.C.

In Costa Rica, 1984, at the request of President Luis Monge

Peking, 1986. Conferring with Zhu Xuefan, Vice President of the Kuomintang

At home, Knebworth, England

we are reading. Fred goes less often to meet the boys at the harbor. He seems to enjoy being with me.

* * * * *

I had so much to tell Bill when he came down to Cornwall last weekend. He saw right away that I was happier.

We discussed many deep things. It was painful to open them up. Bill had silently accepted what had happened to me, but I know he had suffered deeply.

'I think I was wrong to accept your going home,' he said at one point. He felt that Frank, who was old, sick and blind by then, might have got a false impression of me. 'You didn't do anything wrong. You were trying to be responsible.'

'But that's not the point,' I said, 'It was my attitude and motives that were wrong. Worst of all, after the explosion, I covered everything up and pretended all was well again.'

'I should have spoken up,' Bill said. 'I should have talked to Frank.'

I told him about my new relationship with Fred, which moved him deeply.

'I was away too much that last year in America,' he said.

In so many ways, Bill is a firm, straightforward man, who faces difficulties head on. But we realised as we talked, that we share a tendency to defer to those in authority.

I could see he felt guilty that he had not spoken up.

'Many people find it hard to understand how anyone from the British working class really feels,' he said at one point. 'A person from that background *always* feels inferior and insecure.'

We were both silent, our hearts very full.

* * * * *

The days are getting brighter and brighter. Spring is really here now, and there is spring in my heart as well.

It is a joy to open my eyes in the morning, to begin the

day hearing the hissing and pounding of the sea, and then to look through the window at the breathtaking view of water. The sea has become a companion; watching it and hearing it and knowing it is always there brings something strong and tough into my soul. It brings a sense of proportion as well.

Every day when I go out into the lane that runs along beside the sea I feel that I am beginning to walk more erect – to stand up straight and face the world.

February 1964 – Porthleven

A whole year has passed, a year in which I seem to have been reborn and to have found myself again. I know I have a new smiling face. I am healthy and strong. I am in love with Cornwall and the sea.

Fred is bending his mind to his work at last. And he is discovering England through history and literature.

The other day we discussed the future with his headmaster.

'You could go to an English university,' he said calmly as he carved the Sunday joint. That sounded wild to me.

'I think I'll go back to America when I finish school here,' said Fred.

'You could go to Oxford,' John Guise continued. 'Oxford still stands for something in the world.'

That sounded even more fanciful and far-fetched.

But the English school is already doing wonders for Fred. Books have meant so much in my life – they opened up the world for me. Here in this lovely Cornish fishing village, they are beginning to do the same for him. In America his life was all restless activity – always on the go. Now what I have longed for him is beginning to happen.

We discussed Hamlet the other day. Fred said he was intrigued by his personality and his dilemma. Then he mentioned Keats, a gift from Heaven! To be able once again, with my own son, to read those ardent, passionate lines –

to savor the images, the impressions, the unrequited longing, the genius!

In these unexpected gifts, I feel God's love. His presence seems to be flooding in all around me – in the power and roar of the sea, in the spring flowers, in the gulls diving and screeching all day long, and, above all, in this awakening in our son to the unseen territory of the heart and soul. I feel a healing balm.

March 1987 – Knebworth, Hertfordshire

Twenty-three years have gone by since that time of rebirth in Cornwall. For the last fourteen we have lived in the village of Knebworth, thirty miles due north of London.

Our little red brick house, three up and three down, with its casement windows, was given us by two friends, Paul and Madeline Petrocokino. My friendship with Madeline goes back to those early days as a secretary in America when she warned me about Bill's capacity for hard work!

Our long living-room has floor to ceiling bookshelves on either side of the fireplace. For the first time since our marriage all our books are unpacked and lined up together – more than three thousand of them. They include some of my childhood favorites, books on American history from my father's library, and my own collection of the works of Henry James. Bill's books are of quite a different order – political biographies, histories of world labor unions and leaders, and an extensive array of books on current affairs.

We left Cornwall in 1964, living first in Sussex before moving to Hertfordshire. During that time Fred graduated from school and then took degreees from Southampton and Oxford Universities. So the headmaster was right after all.

After looking for a job, Fred finally entered the Civil Service and acquired a small flat in London.

A few years later he married an English girl, Joan, a lecturer in English Literature at one of the Polytechnics. Recently she has taken a post-graduate course in computer sciences, which from now on she will integrate into her arts lectures. It was a common love of opera, especially Wagner, that brought them together.

This marriage has been a delight to us, since our daughter-in-law is gifted in many directions: love of literature and music, a talented gardner and cook and a real home-maker who has decorated their seventeenth century cottage in Kent with great charm. All this has shaken Fred loose from his city ways and allowed him to discover the heady joys of country life. He has even become a keen gardner himself. For the last two years he has been Assistant Private Secretary to the Leader of the House of Lords, and to the Chief Whip.

But before I continue, there is one more development that I need to chronicle.

By 1965 I had been traveling for thirty-four years. Not a week went by in all that time without letters from my parents. Nor had I missed a week in writing to them.

I began to notice that their handwriting was becoming really shaky and my father's letters were filled increasingly with anxiety about mother's health.

My two brothers, as well, had been writing worrying letters, urging me to pay a visit and judge for myself, since I'd not seen my parents since we left for Cornwall. Warner had been married for some time now – another beautiful sister-in-law, a water-color artist. They lived far away in Arizona, so quite a burden had fallen on Arthur, living nearby in Germantown. Art had continued to work with the Quakers and in recent years had done a pioneering work in prison reform in the state of Pennsylvania.

*   *   *   *   *

And so I decided to cross the ocean again, leaving Bill and Fred to fend for themselves.

July–October 1965 – Germantown

They were waiting to greet me – standing in the doorway together. I saw immediately how they had both aged. Dad's huge frame was quite bent. Mother looked tiny, she seemed to have shrunk.

I took them in my arms and we went into the apartment together and closed the door. Dad went to his chair, sank down in it, covered his eyes and broke into shaking sobs.

'Thank God thee has come,' he said, finally.

* * * * *

I returned to England after four months and for the next three years commuted back and forth across the Atlantic.

July 1968–January 1969 – Germantown

In September 1967 I had a cable from Arthur to say that Dad had had a stroke, and was in the intensive care department of the hospital. He was nearly ninety.

When he was fit enough to return home, he needed care round the clock, which meant three nurses, something we could not afford to keep up for long.

So I was off again. I arrived last week to find Aunt Marion in town. She says I must be open to my parents going into a nursing home. I can't accept this. It seems so sad to me that not one of their three children can take them in.

At night, when I stood between their beds, praying and hearing their prayers, I found myself wishing that their hearts would stop beating; that God would take them. If only I could be with them at the end. . . .

* * * * *

Mother is in hospital, after a fall on Christmas Day. She is shocked and unaware of what is going on.

Arthur told me this morning that a room is available in a Quaker nursing home, and so I feel I have to agree. I have been away from Bill and Fred for six months now.

But how will I tell Dad? I know he keeps hoping that

somehow they can be looked after in their own home, that there will be a miracle. Yet he knows as well that I cannot stay indefinitely.

*　*　*　*　*

By eleven o'clock this morning Dad had been dressed by the nurse and was in his study. The sun was shining in the windows. I went in and sat down beside him.

'A room has become vacant in the nursing home,' I said. 'Should we take it?'

Our eyes met, then he turned his face away and gazed out of the window, bringing his hands together over his chest. I could feel a hundred thoughts and emotions racing through his mind. In a moment he looked back at me and smiled gently. We both knew what the answer would be.

'So this is it after all,' he said. 'It's time to go.'

September 1970 – London

I was cooking dinner in one of the MRA houses when someone called me to the telephone. The operator said it was from Philadelphia. A warning?

'Hello,' I said.

I heard my sister-in-law Mary's voice, very clear across 3,000 miles.

'Dear,' she said. 'Dad died very suddenly last night.'

I listened. Strange how the words sank in, words I had been braced for all these years.

The funeral is to be next Tuesday.

I hung up the phone and stood in the passageway. I prayed.

Bill is abroad and will not be able to get to the funeral.

September 1970 – Philadelphia

After the funeral yesterday, Warner suggested that he and I might go to Eagles Mere for a few days. I was so grateful for this suggestion.

222

It was dark by the time we arrived. As I prepared for bed, I opened the window. The sweet, pure air blew in and the deep, deep silence, except for a slight sighing from the nearby pine trees.

I was thinking of my husband, my son, my mother. I was thinking of Dad lying now under the earth.

*   *   *   *   *

We visited our cousins in their cottage nearby and learnt they have decided to sell Eagles Mere. They no longer have the strength and health to keep it up.

So, another ending.

I went for a last walk around the laurel path. It was just the same, but I was swimming in a sea of memories and emotions. I wondered at the power of this place over me. Was it childhood association – a passionate longing and will to stay alive – this clinging to a bit of earth, so searingly beautiful? Was it a tug toward the womb? A desire to melt, to blend, to be absorbed by the pine-needled earth . . . a longing to be at peace?

I wondered if this was a sense of God's being. We are haunted by hints and whispers of an unknown territory, something that hovers and beckons. Even when we have achieved our heart's desire, when we have been able to possess a loved one, or have arrived at the top of all ladders, or have become glitteringly famous – even then there is no rest.

March 1987 – Knebworth

And so I returned to England, to my husband and son. Five years later my mother died. She was almost seven years in the nursing home. Her death, like Dad's, was very sudden. Her heart just stopped beating. So I was not with either of my parents at the end.

Strange, in a way, that after all my earlier reactions I was at last to become a British subject. It was a wrench for a while, and a sadness, when I finally pulled up my American roots and faced the fact that I no longer had an American home. My brothers both live in the United States and I, of course, am always welcome, but nothing can be my home the way my parents' place had been.

However, all these years the multi-faceted subtle character of this ancient kingdom had been creeping slowly into my heart and has gradually taken over completely. It is another love affair – the final one, perhaps.

* * * * *

Looking back over forty years of married life, I can truthfully say that every year seems to deepen my devotion for Bill. I am convinced that he is the only man with whom I could have lived so happily and with such satisfaction.

I feel cherished by Bill, and when I married him, it was as if I had come home.

We certainly have our disagreements and irritations from time to time, but fundamentally we are in harmony. There is a lot of space in our marriage. We don't try to control each other. We don't always do the same things; we are not even interested in all the same things. Yet in our basic approach to life we are quite similar. We each have an individual commitment to do God's will, as far as we can ascertain it, and we have a commitment to each other for life.

What I love most about Bill is his large approach to life. He has high standards, but they are never narrow and legalistic. He seems to be interested in any human being who crosses his path – whether it be the shopkeeper who sells him vegetables, someone he meets on a train, the head of a trade union, a cabinet minister, a corporation president, coal miner or shipyard worker.

I am always moved when I observe how quick Bill is to sense if someone he meets is sad or insecure. Even though he is so busy, he never allows this to stop him giving time to people who are in some kind of need. He is particularly sensitive to shy, inferior people, who find he is more than ready to listen to them, as he draws them out.

Perhaps the only way to understand what makes Bill tick is to realize that for these last fifty years he has had one primary aim – to put as many people as possible in touch with an experience of faith that he feels could, if applied, finally bring about a just society. He tries to bring the best out of people, to give them a big enough idea to live by, so that their public and private lives are in harmony with each other.

We live in an ideological age, bombarded with conflicting ideas. Countries are torn apart through the intensely held convictions of rival groups. Class war is used to stir up envy and bitterness. So much of Bill's work is to help people to think clearly: as he says, 'not right or left or center but in a different dimension altogether.'

Strangely, there are many similarities of background between the two men I have been closest to in my life. Dreiser and Bill both came from a German background; both grew up in extreme poverty, keenly conscious of the realities and suffering in the world. Like Bill, Dreiser had a broad approach to life, and coupled a powerful will with a capacity for great tenderness.

But while Bill's experience of poverty never made him bitter, Dreiser never got over his childhood. He was unable to forget how his mother had toiled to feed her eleven children. Nor could he forget the humiliation he felt, years later, when he tramped the streets looking for a job. These experiences created a hatred of the privileged classes which he never relinquished. Moral Re-Armament harnessed Bill's passion to eliminate these cruel injustices in a commitment which goes much deeper, I believe, than Dreiser's identification with Communism ever did.

As I was finishing this book, I asked an old friend how he would describe Bill. Stuart Smith – a Scot, now an American citizen – is married to Polly Anne, my friend from the days with Annie. He writes of the thirst for knowledge which drives Bill to discover where to buy the out-of-town newspapers in every city he visits; the bulging suitcase of papers and books which accompanies him wherever he travels; his inability to forget a friend; the energy he puts into everything he does. 'He always walks at a swift pace, generally with a bundle of newspapers under his arm,' he writes. 'No hour is too late and no trouble too great for him. He does everything with a gusto that shows he is enjoying every minute of it.'

* * * * *

The last fifteen years have been the busiest of our lives – a crescendo which continues even now in our mid-seventies.

We are still called on to travel extensively. At seventy-seven I don't find it easy to shut up the house and fly to distant lands, yet having done so, I never regret it.

In the last years we have gone annually to the United States and to the summer conferences at the Moral Re-Armament center in Caux, Switzerland. We have made two trips to South Africa and we went to Rhodesia when the war was on and back to Zimbabwe after independence. Bill has made three trips to Czechoslovakia and recently toured South America – Argentina, Brazil, Costa Rica, Chile, Colombia, Uruguay. With his love of statistics, he tells me that during the tour he had individual talks with 144 trade unionists – 'proper' talks, he calls them, not just passing the time of day.

Bill continues to go every year to the ILO in Geneva – which now represents 151 countries and includes every country in the United Nations. His friendships there go back over decades. For forty-two years, for instance, he kept in touch with the Chinese workers' delegate he met at the ILO in Philadelphia in 1944. In 1986, as Vice-Chairman of the Standing Committee of the National People's Congress in China, this man invited Bill to visit his country. Bill spent twelve days there and went on afterwards to Japan and the Philippines.

Another friend through the years has been Dr. P. P. Narayanan from Malaysia, head of the International Federation of Free Trade Unions with its 91 million members. Bill often quotes his favorite sayings: 'We don't need to hate the man we disagree with;' 'Every saint has a past; every sinner has a future.'

*　　*　　*　　*　　*

At home, one of our joys is entertaining all the people who come to see us. Many come for the night and settle down before the fire for long talks. There is hardly a political situation in any country with which Bill is not familiar. Periodicals and newspapers from all over the world, including the Soviet press, come through our letter box – and are stacked, from floor to ceiling, in his 'office'. He has his own system of filing and – amazingly – can put his hands on what he needs. We have an overflow in the garage, cartons of newspaper clippings instead of a car.

What people seem to value is his judgement. He knows his facts, but he doesn't get carried away emotionally as I do on 'hot' issues.

Some of our callers come to discuss situations in their lives which cause them concern. Then all Bill and I have been through can be used to the full to help other people. I can tell them about the freedom which came into my life when I admitted and gave up my hatred, and how these days my heart is filled with gratitude towards Frank, who cared enough to stop me in my tracks when I was going in the wrong direction.

*　　*　　*　　*　　*

Late in life I have become a gardner. I find I have a special passion for roses and we now have forty-six rose bushes, many of them ramblers which climb over the fence and around the windows and the front door.

Bill and I have also developed a real interest in birds.

My great joy is when we can sit in the garden together and watch the birds who come regularly to bathe and drink in the bird bath and to take food from the bird table. I am keen to cultivate the friendship of the shyer birds – the thrush and tits and finches – but Bill is all for the masses. He goes

227

out onto the lawn with a bowl of crumbs and is thrilled when swarms of sparrows and starlings, thirty at a time, cover the grass – the proletariat, as it were!

On summer evenings, there is a thrush who comes out from the beech hedge to take her place on our roof, and there, just at sunset, she sings her heart out. Why does she sing so regularly and sweetly in the evening dusk? I had been discussing the habits of birds with Bill, and when I told him how they sing to claim their territory, he said: 'You mean they don't sing because they are happy?'

I found it difficult to answer. I didn't want to take away from him that childlike belief. Perhaps they *are* happy when they sing. I hope so.

* * * * *

Over and over again I have used the discoveries I made in Cornwall to open other hearts. So many seem to live with hidden bitterness, unknown even to themselves, needing to hear a story that shines a searchlight into areas that are carefully covered over, so often with a smile, so that the world will think all is well. Underneath there can be breaking hearts. I remember Annie saying to me several times, 'Why are you so nice on the outside?' I didn't really understand what she meant, but I certainly do now.

Since those Cornwall years I have also met parents whose ambition for their children has been thwarted when the children have decided to go another way. In some there has been a withdrawal of affection or a silent judgement that has created hurt on both sides. As Bill and I tell our story, many parents have been able to re-establish contact.

I think that the most enriching and satisfying experience is to find that, through God's love and grace, one can be used – even in a small way – to help other people to find release and fulfillment.

And these days, too, my thoughts turn to my father of a Sunday evening sitting at the piano singing – 'And on His shoulder gently laid and home rejoicing brought me.'

This has been my journey and my education.

PICTURE ACKNOWLEDGEMENTS

All pictures are personal photographs belonging to the Clark and Jaeger families, with the exception of the following:

General Wayne (from an engraving by H. B. Hall & Sons, New York)
Theodore Dreiser portrait (Culver Pictures)
Cleve Hicks (MRA Archive)
Madison Square Gardens (Paul Popper)
With my typewriter (Arthur Strong)
Cavalcade of cars (Arthur Strong)
Frank Buchman (MRA Archive)
Henry Ford Memorial Hospital (Arthur Strong)
Street in Stockport (Arthur Strong)
Meeting in East London (MRA Archive)